Beading—
the
Creative Spirit

Finding Your *Sacred* Center through the Art of *Beadwork*

Walking Together, Finding the Way®
SKYLIGHT PATHS®
PUBLISHING
Woodstock, Vermont

Beading—The Creative Spirit:
Finding Your Sacred Center through the Art of Beadwork

2009 Quality Paperback Edition, First Printing
© 2009 by Wendy Ellsworth

Library of Congress Cataloging-in-Publication Data
Ellsworth, Wendy, 1948–
  Beading : the creative spirit : finding your sacred center through the art of beadwork / Wendy Ellsworth ; project photographs by David Ellsworth.—Paperback ed.
      p. cm.
  Includes bibliographical references and index.
  ISBN-13: 978-1-59473-267-6 (quality pbk.)
  ISBN-10: 1-59473-267-1 (quality pbk.)
  1. Beadwork. I. Title.
  TT860.E47 2009
  745.594'2—dc22

                                                                    2009024916

10 9 8 7 6 5 4 3 2 1
Manufactured in the United States of America
Cover art: *Beaded Prayer Pouch*, *Ruffled Cabochon Brooch*, *Chakra Necklace*, *Geometric Mandala*, and *Prayer Beads for Barack Obama* by Wendy Ellsworth.
Cover design: Melanie Robinson
Cover and interior photographs: David Ellsworth
Computer graphics for project diagrams: Ed Fromhagen
Hand-drawn illustrations: F. L. Hanisch

> SkyLight Paths Publishing is creating a place where people of different spiritual traditions come together for challenge and inspiration, a place where we can help each other understand the mystery that lies at the heart of our existence.
>
> SkyLight Paths sees both believers and seekers as a community that increasingly transcends traditional boundaries of religion and denomination—people wanting to learn from each other, *walking together, finding the way.*

SkyLight Paths, "Walking Together, Finding the Way," and colophon are trademarks of LongHill Partners, Inc., registered in the U.S. Patent and Trademark Office.

Walking Together, Finding the Way®
Published by SkyLight Paths Publishing
A Division of Longhill Partners, Inc.
Sunset Farm Offices, Route 4, P.O. Box 237
Woodstock, VT 05091
Tel: (802) 457-4000   Fax: (802) 457-4004
www.skylightpaths.com

*This book is lovingly dedicated
to my husband,
David*

CONTENTS

ACKNOWLEDGMENTS

I offer thanks to the Creator for my life, for the Creative Spirit that moves through me, and for the mysteries of the universe that continually fill me with inspiration.

I offer thanks to all my teachers, both from the Shadow and the Light. In particular, I wish to acknowledge Sant Kirpal Singh, Nancy Doyne, Chico, Barbara Ann Brennan, Jane Winyoté Ely, Kay Cordell Whitaker, Wind Daughter, Shirley Khabbaz, Kofi Opoku, the Pebble Hill School of Sacred Ministries, my parents, children, grandchildren, and my sweet husband, David. I would not be who I am today without your help and guidance.

To my soul sister, Rebecca Lolosoli, and the fearless Samburu women of Umoja Oaso Woman's Village in Archer's Post, Kenya: I offer you special thanks of gratitude for all that you have taught me, for your courage, your resilience, your infectious joy, your unwavering support and belief in basic human rights, and your love of beading. You have touched my heart at the deepest level, and I will continue to support you in your efforts to not only survive but to thrive.

I offer my gratitude for the help I have received from the following people who have supported me through the process of manifesting this book into reality:

To Ric Hanisch, for your hand-drawn illustrations, your many years of friendship, and your commitment to the Creative Spirit. You continue to be an inspiration to all who know and love you.

To Ed Fromhagen, for your computer graphics of all the beaded projects. Your willingness over the years to help me with the graphics for the projects I have designed is much appreciated, along with your delightful sense of midwestern humor.

To Marcia Broucek, who first called me to ask if I would be interested in writing this book (on my sixtieth birthday, no less), then proceeded to edit it for me. Thank you for keeping my writing on target, for reminding me that "less is more," for asking lots of good questions, and for believing in this book.

To Emily Wichland, vice president of Editorial and Production, and the staff at SkyLight Paths, whose help in the final stages of editing completed the process of its manifestation. Thank you also for your belief in this book and for your guidance throughout this project.

To Joyce J. Scott, "Queen Mother" of seed bead artists: Thank you for your fearlessness and commitment to the Creative Spirit and your dedication to developing beading into a contemporary art form. You single-handedly opened the doors for the rest of the field to go through. Thank you for allowing me to use an image of *Head Shot* for this book.

To Karen Paust, bead artist extraordinaire: Thank you for your friendship and for your love of the natural beauty that exists in abundance all around us. Your ability to capture the essence of that beauty through your beadwork is inspirational to everyone who sees it, as evidenced in *Polyphemous Moth*. Thank you for allowing me to feature an image of this. You are as beautiful as the flowers you patiently bead in size 24 seed beads!

To NanC Meinhardt, master teacher and free-form bead artist: Thank you for your dedication to teaching and to singing your Song through the art of beadwork. Your work has inspired beaders all over the world. Thank you for allowing me to use your remarkable piece *Mother Load* as an example in the book. I just wish she could have been shown in color!

To JoAnn Baumann, another bead artist singing her own Song: Thank you for your willingness to explore your life through your bead art and sharing it with the world. I appreciate being able to show *Not This One* in the book.

To Gail Gorlitzz, sculptor and artist who is using beading as her art form: thank you so much for letting me have an image of *Eye Sea* for the book.

To Susan Strong, lampwork bead artist: Thank you for sending me an image of one of your sacred glass hearts to include in the book.

To Dustin Wedekind, a.k.a. "Bead Boy": Thank you so much for the image of your archetypal snake goddess sculpture, *Ungud* (*Snake Goddess*).

To Joyce Tannian, director of Water is Life—Kenya: Thank you for loaning me your rosary to photograph for the book and for your commitment to helping the Amboseli Maasai. I share your love, passion, and concern for the country of Kenya and for the Maasai people in particular.

To my sons, Isaac and Adrian Kennedy, and daughter, Kate Ellsworth: thank you for your love and support throughout this project.

To my granddaughter Melanie: I am so happy you share my love of beading and thank you for all the hidden love notes you left for me to discover while I was working on the book.

To my beloved husband, David: Thank you for all your patience and help during this project, and special thanks for your skills in photographing all the projects and examples of beadwork for this book. You set a remarkable bar when it comes to living from a place of authenticity and personal integrity, inspired by the Creative Spirit. Thank you for keeping me grounded while I worked on this book and in everyday life in general. I love, appreciate, and adore you.

INTRODUCTION

Two roads diverged in a wood, and I—
I took the one less traveled by,
And that has made all the difference.
　　　　—Robert Frost, "The Road Not Taken"

Beading and my spiritual path are intricately interwoven. It would be difficult for me to separate the two because they are so completely intertwined with one another. As I sit and weave with my beads, I allow the Creative Spirit to flow through me, and though my hands are doing the work, another force is actively participating in the process. This force is a transmission of Spirit that fills me with deep inner peace and joy as I bead. As a result, the practice of my art form has become a creative path to my sacred center.

Many people resist the terms *Spirit* or *spirituality*, perhaps confusing them with religion if they have turned away from a church or a particular set of religious teachings. My references to using beads for spiritual inspiration have nothing to do with organized religion. It is my belief that Spirit is the essence of who we are and the source of our creative potential. Spirit is infinite in its potential to flow through us and bring us to a greater awareness of ourselves. It is what we are secretly longing for. Through Spirit, we come to know our purpose in life; we learn the wisdom of our soul's journey and evolution. It is always available to us for guidance, and through it we can learn to live passionately and with greater depth of inner joy.

I feel most connected to my spirituality when I am in the creative process or am outside enjoying the natural world in her infinite mystery and beauty. Whether searching for the elusive pink lady's slipper orchid or observing underwater sea life, I have always turned to nature as a source of spiritual and artistic inspiration.

As we live through these tumultuous times, with seemingly every institution in our culture in crisis, we may wonder where to turn for comfort or guidance. I propose that we turn to the work of our hands, that we pick up our needles and thread and weave with our beads as we allow the Spirit of Creativity to move within us. Through this process, we can reconnect with our wholeness, our meaning and purpose for being, here and now. We can find our center and "re-member" what it feels like to be at peace within ourselves. When we are in touch with our center, we will be in a more balanced position to deal with the unexpected twists and turns in our journey through life, especially during this time of uncertainty.

It took many years for me to be able to comprehend all the ways that beading guided my spiritual journey. It did not happen overnight. Rather, it happened over time, and the story of my journey is woven throughout this book. Looking back, I can see the stages that I processed through in my beadwork and how they were a mirror reflection of the inner work I was doing.

It is my hope that as you read the book and make the bead projects for yourself, you will not only enjoy the beauty of your creations but also be able to use the material as a tool for your own spiritual growth. Each chapter has an exercise in addition to a meditative practice for you to choose from as well as two beading projects that relate to the chapter themes. The first project in each chapter is geared toward novice beaders, and the second is aimed at intermediate and more advanced beaders. Each of the projects has photographs and diagrams to help you along the way. (I have written this book with the assumption that my readers will have a basic understanding and working knowledge of off-loom bead weaving. If you are a beginner, there are several books listed in the Resources section at the back of the book that can help you with the basics or provide some coaching if you get stuck.) Each of the projects is also shown in color in the color insert in the middle of the book.

This is neither a "how-to" craft book nor a "coffee table" book. It is a workbook focused on how you can use beading to find your sacred center. I have been teaching classes in off-loom bead weaving since the early 1980s, designing fun and interesting projects for students to make using the different bead weaving stitches that I have taught myself. My teaching arose from the desire to share my knowledge and expertise with others, with the hope of inspiring them to experiment and explore new ideas on their own. Some of my students have shared with me how profoundly they have been affected by what they have learned about themselves on a deeper spiritual level while they were beading. Similar to my own experiences, these students have continued to use beading to access their sacred center within, leading them to a place of greater inner peace and calm. I believe that the renaissance of interest in beading over the past fifteen years is directly attributed to its beneficial meditative aspects—as well as how much fun it is!

Chapter 1 explores the power of the mandala as a means of creative expression. I spent ten years making beaded mandalas, and they are what started my passion and love of beading. Beading mandalas can guide us to our center and help us achieve a balance between the right and left hemispheres of our brains, which leads to greater peacefulness and inner joy. The projects for this chapter include directions for creating a beaded Geometric Mandala as well as a Personal Mandala. These are not difficult to make, and a novice beader will be able to complete one easily.

Chapter 2 examines how beads have been used for thousands of years for devotion and prayer. The act of beading lends itself to contemplation, and when we bring our conscious awareness to our beadwork, it can become a means of reconnecting with a higher force. The two projects in this chapter show how to make a simple strand of Personal Prayer Beads as well as a Beaded Prayer Pouch in two-bead brick stitch.

Chapter 3 stirs the pot in search of the authentic self. Being fully present in the here and now of beading can assist us in achieving this. I look at the archetypes of Wild Woman and the Goddess and their importance to contemporary women's lives. The first project is a Goddess Archetype Necklace in spiral rope chain stitch; the second is a Beaded Stick Figure Goddess in gourd stitch.

Chapter 4 focuses on the ancient theory of the chakra system and how we can use the two vertical currents of core energy flowing through the body. I outline some of the characteristics of each of the seven chakras and show how I used each chakra as a process for designing beaded imagery. The projects for this chapter include a Chakra Necklace that uses the colors of the chakra system in spiral rope chain stitch and a multilayered Chakra Flower Sculpture in flat circular gourd stitch

Chapter 5 explores playing with light and color to shake up our palette. I review the major color theories and look at how surface finishes on glass beads affect the way colors interact with each other, as well as how our eyes will perceive them. The first project is a Free-form Gourd Stitch Bracelet that can challenge you to work with colors you normally would not choose to combine. The second project is a Ruffled Cabochon Brooch with radical increases in gourd stitch that cause the beads to ruffle and undulate in 3-D.

Chapter 6 explores the Spirit of Creativity and how we can use this innate force for personal expression and spiritual inspiration. I introduce ten tools of creative expression and how we can apply them to our lives and to our beading. I also examine five cripplers of creative expression and how they can prevent us from reaching our full, creative potential. Both of the projects for this chapter involve working with the universal symbol of the spiral: a Dutch Spiral Necklace and a free-standing Spiral Vessel in gourd stitch.

The final chapter examines what it means to bead our bliss and sing our Song. I explore ten "beads" of our personal Song that enable us to express ourselves. The projects for this chapter include directions for making Song Beads in flat-weave gourd stitch and a beautiful embellished coral reef cuff with freshwater pearls in my favorite stitch, known as herringbone or Ndebele.

It has been a humbling experience for me to put into words how beading has become a meditative, spiritual practice for me over time. In writing this book, I revisited authors I have read over the years for guidance. I have drawn on the many workshops and classes I have taken for personal growth, all of which have contributed to my search for meaning and purpose. And yet I keep coming back to the beading itself. It has been the constant current flowing through every developmental stage I have gone through. It has been my companion through many a "dark night of the soul" and has kept me going through the most difficult times in my life.

Beads have been my best friend, partner, muse, therapist, and, on rare occasions, my antagonist. They have provided me with direction in life, a way of reconnecting with the center of my soul, and great joy and bliss. My hope, as I share my passion, is to provide fuel for your journey into the world of beading and spirituality. May the currents of this beautiful art form renew your faith and trust in the healing power of the Creative Spirit.

Find Your Center

For Equilibrium and Balance

> *God is a sphere whose center is everywhere and whose circumference is nowhere.*
>
> —Hermes Trismegistus

What Is a Bead?

What comes to mind when you think of a bead? Most likely you picture contemporary beads that are manufactured by glass factories in the Czech Republic, Japan, China, or India. However, beads have been around for a very long time and have been made in an enormous variety of materials other than glass.

Lecturer, curator, and author Lois Sherr Dubin, in her groundbreaking book *The History of Beads: From 30,000 B.C. to the Present*, shows many examples of beads that have been documented as far back as 38,000 BCE. The earliest known beads were excavated in a cave in France; made from grooved animal teeth and bones, they had clearly been worn as pendants. Our hominid ancestors probably used these early forms of beads as talismans. Perhaps they believed that by wearing parts of the animals they hunted, they would gain power over them, or perhaps they wore beads as a way

Loose beads.

Czech glass seed beads.

of praying for protection from the very dangerous animals they were hunting. At the very least, there was obvious symbolic meaning to these early beads that were so treasured they were deliberately buried in a secluded cave long ago.

Our early human ancestors made beads out of many of the natural materials that were available in their environment, including seeds, shells, animal bones, berries, wood, and other vegetal matter. By 4000–2000 BCE, beads were being made out of hard stones such as agate, carnelian, jasper, lapis lazuli, and fossilized coral. Because of the volume of beads that have been excavated in archaeological sites from this period, I speculate that these ancient people had become as obsessed with the making and wearing of beads as some of us still are today. Beads had become objects of personal adornment, indicators of social status, as well as important items of trade and currency, all of which continue to be relevant today. Within a contemporary context, beads are enjoying a renaissance of interest, and many people are rediscovering the joys of using them to make exciting and dynamic new art forms.

Anything with a hole in it that can be threaded with some kind of stringing material could be considered a bead. While I have occasionally used beads made from natural materials, my primary beading materials have been small glass beads known as seed beads. All the projects for this book incorporate their use, so I want to give a brief explanation of how they are made.

Glass seed beads are traditionally manufactured using two primary methods. The first is known as *drawn glass,* made by forming a hollow "gather" of molten glass that is then stretched or drawn out into a long, thin tube. Over the centuries this method evolved from a manual process of two glass workers pulling a glass tube progressively thinner by walking away from each other into a continuously running mechanical process capable of producing hundreds of these long tubes per hour. This long tube is later cut into smaller tubes whose rough edges are softened or rounded by tumbling or reheating, producing what is now called a seed bead.

The second method dates from antiquity and involves winding molten glass multiple times around a coated mandrel of metal. This type of bead is called *lampworked* because in the early 1600s the beads were made by winding molten glass over oil lamps. Some seed beads from India and China are still being produced using this method. Contemporary lampworked beads could be considered large-scale examples of this method.

In the 1980s, computer control of seed bead manufacturing came into play, both in the Czech Republic and in Japan. The Japanese invented a new process for making glass seed beads that involved cutting the glass with lasers. Computers control the extruding process and continuously produce beads with very accurate diameters and hole sizes. These beads are made in a variety of shapes, the most popular being cylindrical, and have large holes that make beading with them a delight.

Contemporary lampworked glass beads.

Toho Japanese seed beads.

My Introduction to Beading

Many of my beading students have asked me how and when I chose to start beading as a career. It involves a love story, so that is where I will begin.

In February 1970, I met an intriguing man who lived in an old mining cabin high up in the mountains. He lived a simple life with few amenities (he had no running water or electricity), and he made beaded leather handbags as a profession. Visiting him in his little cabin, I soon felt a strong connection to him and to the wilderness in which he lived. It represented a freedom I had never known and was drawn to.

After college graduation, I decided to join him, and soon found myself living at 10,500 feet on the back side of Aspen Mountain. The personal freedom I experienced was intoxicating. During the days I explored the high country, and in the evenings, by the light of kerosene lamps, I learned how to bead circular mandalas that I laced onto leather and made into purses. For the first time in my life, I was creating a piece of artwork with my own hands! When each purse was finished, we took them down the mountain to Aspen and sold them, usually through the Gypsy Woman, a store that still exists and has hardly changed in all these ensuing years.

I was in love with the man, with the mountains, with my new-found freedom, with my persona as a "mountain woman"—and, above all, with my new skill at beading. At that time I had no idea how far beading would take me; I was young, searching for meaning and purpose, and had a lot of spiritual questions. In many ways, beading provided the spiritual connection I was longing for as it led me gently back home to myself.

To say that this was a radical change for me is an understatement of grand proportions!

My parents thought I had dropped off the face of the planet, and they could not understand what had possessed their college-educated, debutante daughter to make such a choice for herself. From my perspective, and from the perspective of time, I can unequivocally say that I was in exactly the place I needed to be in order to learn the lessons I was ready for. I had gone to the edge of the cliff and leaped; courage, trust, and faith rose up to greet me, and I flew with wings of passion and determination. I would not trade that year with any other year of my life. As the Zen Buddhist proverb teaches: "Before Enlightenment, chop wood, carry water. After Enlightenment, chop wood, carry water!"

These many years later, I am still beading, chopping wood, and carrying water. And I am still making mandalas.

The Power of the Mandala

The word *mandala* comes from the ancient Sanskrit language of India and can be translated as meaning "circle, center, or circumference." Mythologist Joseph Campbell, in his book *The Power of Myth,* described a mandala as a circle that is coordinated or symbolically designed so that it has the meaning of a cosmic order. Campbell went on to say that when we create a mandala, we are attempting to align our own circle of life with the universal circle of creation. He thought that making mandalas was a discipline for pulling the scattered aspects of our lives together, for finding a center and ordering ourselves to it.

Afghan beaded mandala, c. 1960, maker unknown.

These ideas are mirrored in the work of Carl Jung, the Swiss psychiatrist who is credited with reintroducing the intrinsic power of creating healing mandalas to westerners. Jung felt that mandalas could be used as a therapeutic aid for patients in their search for what he termed their "individuation." Exploring our uniqueness, or individuality, Jung believed, could bring us back into wholeness and unity with the Self.

The circle seems to be a universal emblem. Ancient prehistoric peoples felt compelled to draw circles and spirals in their rock art in Africa, Europe, North America, and Australia. Though the meaning of these ancient circles may be a mystery, we do not have to look very far into historic times and into the present to see that the circle represents wholeness, unity, and harmony. People still connected to their ancient wisdom truths and to the earth-based traditional spiritual teachings of their ancestors consider life as a circle, and for them the mandala is symbolic

Maasai mandala, Kenya, 2004, maker unknown.

of this circle of life and death, the cosmic procession of the planets and stars, and the earthly seasons and galactic cycles.

In Tibetan Buddhism, there is a tradition of creating mandalas called *thangkas* that are visual representations of the sacred scriptures of tantric Buddhism. They are created by monks who must first enter into a prayerful state through chanting and meditation. The monks train and study for many years in order to replicate the exact way to draw the sacred images of these mandalas; there is no room for improvisation. They consider these mandalas symbolic patterns of light and sound that reflect the evolution of the universe, and they see *thangkas* as a sacred art form.

Tibetan monks living in exile often travel to raise money for their monasteries by creating magnificent sand mandalas. Each mandala is a flat, two-dimensional painting made of loose sand in a palette of cotton candy pastel colors. Tibetan monks, in a state of meditation, sit on the floor and sift fine streams of colored sand through metal funnels to create the complex and symbolic designs of the mandala. In Tibetan Buddhist thought, creation of a sand mandala is said to effect purification and healing on three levels of meaning. On the outer level, the mandala represents the world in its divine form; on the inner level, it represents a map by which the ordinary human mind is transformed into an enlightened mind; and on the secret level, it depicts the perfect balance of the subtle energies of the body and the clear light dimension of the mind. Buddhism teaches that within each person is the seed of enlightenment, and this seed may be nourished by contemplating a mandala. Those who view or help create a mandala may gain profound spiritual insight and experience a sense of deep inner peace.

I once had the opportunity to witness the creation of a Tibetan sand mandala at my interfaith church. Monks from the Drepung Loseling Monastery constructed the mandala over a period of five days. As I sat beside them, watching them create this mandala and listening to the sound of the metal sticks rubbing along the metallic funnels in conjunction with the monks' atonal chanting, I felt transported to another place and time. I was overwhelmed at the beauty and perfection of the completed mandala; it was breathtakingly colorful and symbolically meaningful. At the closing ceremony, they consecrated the mandala with chanting, singing, and meditation. I knew that the colored sands that had been used to make the mandala would be swept away when the ceremony was finished, to symbolize the Buddhist belief in the impermanence of life. However, I was not prepared for my reaction to watching this stunning creation be swept away with a small whisk broom. I spontaneously started crying and could not stop the tears. As an artist, I hope my beaded creations will last for many years, and I strive for museum-quality work; yet what I was witnessing was the opposite of what I work so hard to achieve. It was an incredible lesson in the importance of being in the present, of letting go, surrendering, and knowing that nothing is permanent.

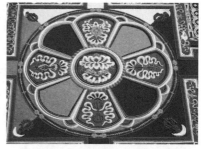

Detail, Chenrezig sand mandala made by monks from Drepung Gomang Monastery, Doylestown, Pennsylvania, 2007. (Photograph by Greg Schultz)

In North America, Navajo sand paintings are also created in the form of mandalas as a sacred, healing art form. The Navajo term for sand painting is *iikaah*, which translates into "the place where the gods come and go." A *hataalii*, or medicine man or woman, constructs the sand painting on the ground using pigments made from ground-up natural stones, charcoal, pollen, cornmeal, and perhaps crushed flowers. The holy people are then summoned to enter the sand painting to infuse it with their healing powers. A person feeling out of balance or out of harmony can request this ceremony as a Healing Way, a healing path that can lead back to a state of wholeness.

There are also many examples of mandalas in Gothic cathedrals in Europe and the United States. The magnificent circular stained glass rose windows that face toward the west in these Christian churches are meant not only to remind us of beauty, both internal and external, but also to symbolize our connection to the universal cosmos. There are also examples of mandalas in the circular labyrinths of these cathedrals, often designed in floor tiles near the entrance of the church. The labyrinth at Chartres Cathedral in France is perhaps the most famous of these; many contemporary venues, including my own church, have also constructed labyrinths for meditation. Some people see walking a labyrinth as a bridge from the mundane to the Divine. Others experience the wandering path as taking us to the center of ourselves. Kathy Doore, an author of books on sacred spaces, describes moving through a labyrinth as a way of "chang[ing] ordinary ways of perception connecting the inner and the outer, the right brain and the left brain."

Our left brain is detail oriented. By putting details into a linear configuration, our left brain gives us the concept of time, of past, present, and future. It breaks down the "bigger picture" into minute parts that it can describe and define. The left brain is where our sense of individuality lives and where we compare ourselves to others. It is where we develop judgment and learn to analyze factual knowledge.

Our right brain allows us to live in the present moment, where we can think intuitively, outside the box, and creatively explore the possibilities each new moment brings. The right brain is where our artistic juices can flow freely without inhibition or judgment. Rules and regulations do not exist in the right hemisphere of our brain. To our right brain, the moment of *now* is the only time that exists.

The amazing thing about these two sides of our brains is that they work together to accomplish just about every action we take. We need both sides of our brain to work in harmony with one another. But for most of us, it takes tremendous work to slow down the incessantly chattering "monkey mind" of our left brain to come fully into the present moment and to remind ourselves of what it feels like to play in the creative process. Beading can be a means of doing this. And beading mandalas in particular can help us achieve this balance.

For me, creating beaded mandalas is a means of reconnecting with my internal center and exploring a new path to spiritual and creative expression. During my "mountain years" of beading circular mandalas, I would start each one with a single bead stitched in the center of a piece of leather stretched on an embroidery hoop. That placement of a single bead was an act of centering in the moment. From there, I would proceed to play in the creative process by adding beads of different colors to form the primarily geometric patterns of the mandala. Each day I would look at the beads in their rainbow hues and ask myself which color or colors I needed to work with that day, as well as what colors the mandala needed for its overall pattern and design. Using this interactive process, bringing right-brain sensing into balance with left-brain activity, I would then choose a color palette to work with.

As I think about the many mandalas I beaded during that ten-year period, I would now describe the process as a means for accessing my sacred center.

Finding Your Sacred Center

According to ancient Eastern religious belief systems, there is a center located in our bodies that is a *spiritual* center. This is called the Third Eye or spiritual eye, and it is located at the midpoint between the eyebrows, deep in the brain. It is believed that through this Third Eye center we can perceive the inner light of God and the ultimate spiritual reality of oneness and wholeness. (I'll say much more about this Third Eye in chapter 4 when we look at the chakra system of the body.)

There is also a place in our bodies that is our *physical* center, or what is called a "still point within." The martial art forms of tai chi and qigong work with this centering point and call it the place where our chi, or energy, resides. Another term for this point is the Tan T'ien. In the tai chi tradition, all movement and meditation originates from this focal point in the body. It is our physical center of gravity, located in the middle of the belly, approximately two to three inches below the navel. It is this point of equilibrium that a dancer must connect with as she leaps from place to place and still remains balanced. It is the place that Sufi whirling dervishes must center on in order to spin for hours in trance. When we are centered in this spot, we can move outwardly from a place of focused power and strength.

Centering ourselves brings us back into equilibrium and into balance. In her book *Centering,* ceramic artist M. C. Richards refers to centering as a process of feeling the whole in every part, of gathering together these parts and putting them into some kind of order. Centering brings us into wholeness, and from this place, we can more easily handle the trials and tribulations that life sends our way.

Yet most of us are never taught how to "center" ourselves. It certainly is not taught in our mainstream academic curriculae! We can begin by first becoming *aware* of the concept of centering and how it might feel in our bodies. In my beadworking classes, I often use a short exercise to help people get acquainted with their "center." Stop for just a minute and give it a try. Standing, begin by bringing your awareness into the present moment, and see if you can feel where your Tan T'ien is located in your belly. Find it with your fingers; then close your eyes and imagine your upper body coming into alignment over this spot. Now, try moving from this center by keeping your focus on your Tan T'ien and walking around. Try this first with your eyes closed, then with them open. Do you feel a difference?

Centering with Beaded Mandalas

Creating a beaded mandala is another way to find your sacred center. In her book *Mandala: Luminous Symbols for Healing,* award-winning author and spiritual healer Dr. Judith Cornell offers several encouraging reasons for creating a mandala:

- It has the regenerative and curative power to activate the latent powers of the mind. The meditative process helps to focus and open the heart to the healing power of unconditional love.

- It has a calming and relaxing effect on the mind and body, focusing and strengthening the will to heal.

- It can bring joy as it facilitates the healing of a sense of psychological fragmentation.

- It can make the invisible visible—expressing paradoxical situations or patterns of ultimate reality that can be expressed in no other way.

- It can reveal unity between human existence and the structure of the cosmos, opening up a perspective in which things can be understood as a whole.

- It can give form and expression to an intuitive insight into spiritual truth by releasing the inner light of the soul.

Since beaded mandalas have been such powerful learning tools for me, I would like to share with you directions for making two types of beaded mandalas. The first project, a Geometric Mandala, is geared toward novice beaders, while the second, a Personal Mandala, is aimed at intermediate and more advanced beaders.

Before you start on one of these projects (or any project in this book), make sure you have created a comfortable space in which to work.

EXERCISE

Creating a Comfortable Space

1. If possible, locate a place and space to work in that is quiet and uncluttered. If it is cluttered, you might want to take the time to clean it up first.
2. Sit in a comfortable chair with good back support.
3. Make sure you have plenty of good, full-spectrum light. An Ott light is excellent for beading because it shows true color, is cool rather than hot, and reduces eye fatigue. (Fluorescent

lights generate a frequency that tends to interfere with the normal pulsation of our energy field, and their spectral range can be unhealthy for our energy field, as well.)

4. You may choose to work with your favorite music playing or in silence.

5. A running water fountain can be very soothing to have in your special place and will remind you of Water as one of the five elements.

6. Find a crystal or stone to place near you to remind you of the element of Earth. (The crystal can be cleansed occasionally by soaking in ¼ teaspoon of sea salt and a pint of spring water overnight.)

7. Open a window, if possible, to let in the element of fresh Air.

8. Light a stick of incense or a candle to remind you of the element of Fire.

9. You may also want to smudge yourself and your workspace before you begin to clear the energy. (See "Blessing the Materials," p. 47 for a smudging exercise.)

10. Turn off the television if you have one in your work space!

11. If you can, allocate a specific time period for beading when you will not be distracted by other responsibilities.

12. Give yourself permission to allow your beading to be a "time-out" from your usual daily activities. Let this be an opportunity to open to the power of Presence and see what happens when you bead with present-moment awareness.

Project 1
Geometric Mandala

You do not need any previous experience in beading to make this mandala. It is basically a process of stitching beads onto whatever material you chose for the foundation, using a simple backstitch in some rows and straight stitching in others. The mandala is geometric in design, with colors of beads creating geometric patterns that radiate out from the center in rows.

Detail, *Geometric Mandala*, Wendy Ellsworth, 1993. (For a color photograph of this project, see color plate 1a.)

The point where you stitch your first bead will become the center of your mandala, and it represents the spiritual center within you. From this center, all the beads you add will radiate outward toward the final circumference. You can make your mandala as big or small as you want.

Ask yourself what colors you feel like working with on any given row. They do not need to blend; there is no "right" color to work with. Ask yourself these questions: In this moment, now, what color or colors do I feel like working with? What pattern would I like to make in this row? Then start playing! I have shown one example above of a mandala that I made; your mandala will be different because you will choose your own bead colors and geometric patterns.

CHOOSING MATERIALS

Mandalas can be made using a wide variety of materials. For the purpose of this project, however, I suggest using glass seed beads stitched onto a synthetic leather material called Ultrasuede. You could also use a piece of soft doeskin leather or even heavy wool felt. If using felt, you might want to use a nonwoven polyester substrate backing in order to get the tightness and tensile strength you need when stretching the material on the embroidery hoop. In that case, you would be beading through two layers at the same time. (See the Resources section at the back of the book for suggested sources for purchasing the substrate.)

MATERIALS

- A 6- or 8-inch embroidery hoop
- A piece of Ultrasuede or soft doeskin, large enough to fit on the hoop
- Seed beads in sizes 11 to 8 in multiple colors (You can make your mandala using just one size bead or many different sizes.)
- Sharps short beading needles in sizes to fit through the holes in your beads (I recommend size 12.)
- Silamide thread size A or Nymo thread size B
- Synthetic wax
- Scissors: a small pair with a sharp point, plus a larger pair strong enough to cut the Ultrasuede or leather
- Beading mat
- Ott light or desk lamp
- Pencil
- Lighter or matches

PROJECT PREPARATION

- Gather your beads and other materials and place them beside your work surface.
- Stretch your piece of Ultrasuede or leather on the embroidery hoop. With both parts of the hoop in place over the Ultrasuede, start tightening the edges of the material until it is "drum tight."
- Look at the colors of beads beside your work space. Are you attracted to one of them? Choose one color for the center bead of your mandala.
- Now you are ready to begin to bead.

STEP 1

- Pull off approximately 4 feet of thread and prestretch it by pulling it out between your hands, working your way along its entire length.
- Thread a needle and bring the two ends of the thread together so it is doubled. Tie the ends with an overhand knot.
- Cut the tips of thread with scissors and burn them with a lighter or match. (Be careful that the tips do not burn into the knot.)
- Wax the thread so the two threads stick together as one.

STEP 2

- Using a pencil, place a mark at the approximate center of the material stretched on the hoop. (It does not need to be exact; your "center" is wherever you start.)
- Bring your needle from the back side to the top of the material, coming up through the material just beside the pencil mark that indicates the center point.
- Pick up a single bead in a color of your choice and run it down the thread to the material. Stitch back down through the material to the back. You have just centered your mandala.

STEP 3: BACKSTITCH CIRCLE AROUND CENTER BEAD

- Bring your needle and thread back to the top of the material, approximately one bead width out from the center bead.
- Pick up two beads in the same color as the central bead (or a different color if you prefer), running them down to the base of the thread at the point where it exits the material.
- Laying the beads flat on the surface, stitch down through the material where the second bead ends. From here, you'll be making a circle in backstitch around the center bead, and you can go either clockwise or counterclockwise, whichever feels better to your hands.
- Bring your needle back to the top of the material in the midpoint between the two beads just added and pass the

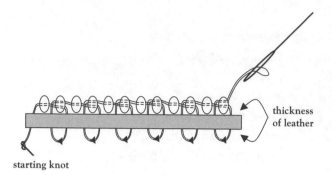

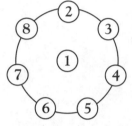

thickness
of leather

starting knot

1.1. Backstitch in a straight line.

1.2. Beads 2–8 are back-stitched every two beads in a circle around a central bead.

needle back through the second bead in the same direction. This is called a backstitch and is illustrated in figure 1.1.

• Now pick up two new beads and run them down the thread so they lie right in front of the bead the thread is coming out of. Stitch down through the material where the second bead ends. Bring your needle back to the top of the material in the midpoint between the two beads just added and backstitch through the second bead in the same direction. You will repeat these two-bead backstitches until you have completed a circle of beads around the center bead. (See figure 1.2.)

• Connect the last bead in your circle to the first one. Stitch down to the back of the material and up to the top side to be in place to begin the next circle of the mandala.

Step 4

• Following step 3, use the backstitch to make at least two or three more circles of beads, radiating out from around the center bead. You can keep the same color or introduce new colors of beads as you make your rows.

Step 5: Spokes

• When you have as many circle rows as you would like, you can begin a row of spokes. Looking at figure 1.3, bring your needle to the top of the material at point A.

• Pick up three beads and stitch down at point B.

• Bring your needle back to the top at point C. Pick up three beads and stitch down at point D.

• Repeat these lines of beads until you have made spokes radiating out around the center in a complete circle, trying to keep the spacing between them somewhat equal. You may begin to introduce a geometric pattern of colors in this step, or just use one color.

STEP 6

- Add a row of beads as a boundary line around the circumference of the spokes you made in step 5 (using the backstitch). You may pick up three beads at a time and stitch back through the third bead in each stitch, or use just two beads per stitch, as in step 3.

STEP 7

- Make a second row of spokes, as in step 5. This time, you might want to pick up four beads per stitch and introduce a geometric pattern by using a contrasting color bead within each spoke that moves one bead up or down each stitch. (See figure 1.4.)

STEP 8

- Repeat step 6.

STEP 9

- Repeat steps 7 and 8 until the mandala is the size you want it to be.
- When making spokes farther out in the diameter of the circle, you can increase the number of beads you pick up per stitch. I have used as many as nine or ten beads per stitch to make the spokes.
- Have fun making geometric patterns with the bead colors. You can refer to color plate 1a, *Geometric Mandalas,* for ideas.
- End with a row of beads in backstitch that goes around the entire outer circumference of the mandala. This border row will create a

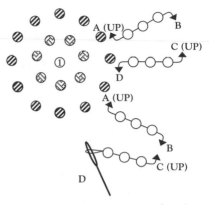

1.3. First row of spokes.

Sample mandala showing boundary row around spokes.

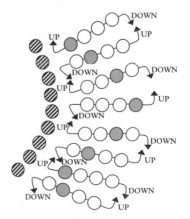

1.4. Second row of spokes, showing geometric bead pattern.

nice boundary line that will contain the energy of the mandala.

STEP 10: FINISHING

Now it is time to take the mandala off the hoop (unless you want to leave it on the hoop and use the hoop as a frame for it). If you'd like to stitch the mandala onto an article of clothing, such as a coat or vest, you will need to first remove it from the hoop:

- Using a sharp pair of scissors or pinking shears, you can cut around the mandala, leaving enough of an edge to stitch through just beside the final row of beads.
- Handstitch the mandala onto the article of clothing.

Another way to finish the mandala would be to glue it, then stitch it onto another piece of fabric or leather, which would become a frame for the piece:

- If you have used leather as the base material, you can cut out a second piece of leather the same size as the mandala and then glue the two pieces together using Barge leather cement. (Be sure to follow the instructions on the Barge tube.)
- Bead an edging around the two pieces of leather, and you can hang your mandala on the wall. (See figures 1.5, 1.6, and 1.7 for three examples of possible edging techniques.)

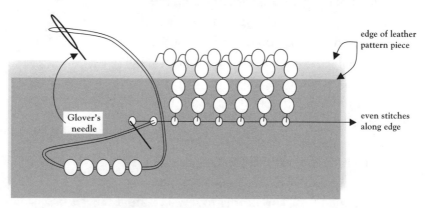

edge of leather pattern piece

Glover's needle

even stitches along edge

1.5. Edge wrapping: whipstitch with beads.

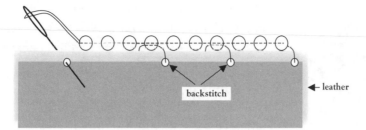

1.6. Beading along a raw edge using backstitch.

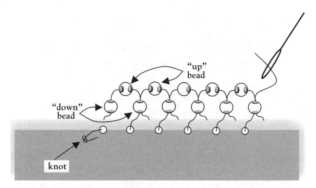

1.7. Basic two-bead edging.

If you want to stitch your mandala onto a piece of fabric:

- Cut a rectangle out of fabric and hem it at the top and bottom.
- You may want to glue the mandala to the fabric before stitching the mandala to the fabric.
- If you have used Ultrasuede or felt as your base material, gluing would work well.
- To hang the piece, you can cut wooden dowels to length, and slide them into the hem at the top and bottom of the fabric.

Another possibility for finishing your mandala would be to stitch it to a piece of fabric and take it to a frame shop where they can make a shadow box for it. You could also use your mandala as a focal point of a purse you make.

◉◉◉

Detail, *Geometric Mandala,*
Wendy Ellsworth, 1993.
(For a color photograph of this
project, see color plate 1a.)

There are many variations on the Geometric Mandala that you can play with as you get comfortable with the methods for making backstitches and spokes. Experiment with different colors, different numbers of rows for each color, shorter or longer spokes. The image featured at left is another mandala I have made that might give you a few ideas about other design possibilities.

Before you begin Project 2, I suggest that you undertake the meditation "Asking for Personal Symbols" to help you open to receiving ideas for symbols that you can use to make your Personal Mandala.

Meditation
Asking for Personal Symbols

1. Sit comfortably in your chair with your feet on the floor and your back straight.
2. Gently close your eyes.
3. Bring yourself into the present moment and take three deep breaths.
4. Watch each breath come in and go out, consciously observing each inhalation and exhalation.
5. With each exhalation, allow the tension in your body to begin to release.
6. Set your responsibilities and duties aside for now; you will return to them later.
7. Gently ask the chatter of your left-brain "monkey mind" to calm down so you can become more fully present in this moment.

8. Relax your jaw, your brow, your shoulders—all places where you hold tension in your body.

9. Notice if there are any other places that are tight or tense; breathe into them consciously in order to release this tightness. Feel yourself lightening up.

10. Bring your attention to your heart area. For just this moment, allow your heart to open to the vibration of love: self-love. Feel your heart begin to soften and become more receptive to receiving this love from and to yourself.

11. Bring your attention up to your Third Eye center, located in the midpoint between your eyebrows.

12. Keeping your attention focused on this spiritual center, imagine this point filled with radiant white light. Allow this light to bless your entire body with its healing energy.

13. Bring your attention back to your Third Eye center and ask to receive a symbol or symbols that represent you at your soul level. Keep breathing consciously and wait for this symbol to appear spontaneously. Be patient; you are in Spirit time.

14. When you receive a symbol and/or feel that the meditation is complete, gently open your eyes and bring your consciousness back into the room.

15. Use a pencil to draw the symbol or symbols on a piece of paper.

16. If you have not received any symbols during your meditation, it is okay. You are surrounded by symbols and perhaps you will be able to find the ones you resonate with in another method of your own choosing.

Personal Mandala

The purpose of this project is to create a mandala of personal expression. You might think of it as a personal shield. However, instead of a heraldic coat of arms, which is inherited and indicates your ancestral lineage, this shield will represent your inner spiritual self.

Detail, *Personal Mandala,*
Wendy Ellsworth, 1989.
(For a color photo of this project, see color plate 1b.)

You may already know some symbols that represent you at your soul level. They may have come to you over time, symbols that you have been drawn to and that seem to represent aspects of yourself that are important to you. I also provide a meditation in this chapter to help you find or explore symbols that have meaning for you. You may prefer another method for bringing these symbols into consciousness. You might walk a labyrinth in search of symbols. Or you might find them through your dreams. You may find that once you start looking for personal symbols, they appear almost magically in your life. Pay attention! Spirit moves in unusual and wondrous ways.

Perhaps the most important thing I can tell you about this Personal Mandala project is that there is no right way or wrong way to create this shield. It will be a spiritual pilgrimage of self-discovery.

MATERIALS

- A 6- or 8-inch embroidery hoop
- Piece of Ultrasuede or soft doeskin, large enough to fit on the hoop
- Seed beads in sizes 11 to 8 in multiple colors (You can make the mandala using just one size bead or different sizes.)

- Sharps short beading needles in sizes to fit through the holes in the beads (I recommend size 12.)
- Silamide thread size A or Nymo thread size B
- Synthetic wax
- Scissors: small pair with sharp point and larger pair strong enough to cut the Ultrasuede or leather
- White paper
- Colored pencils, crayons, markers, or pastels
- Device with which to draw the outer diameter of the circle on your Ultrasuede (This could be a large container lid or plate to trace around; or you could use a compass.)
- Ruler for drawing straight lines
- Beading mat
- Ott light or desk lamp
- Pencil with eraser

PROJECT PREPARATION

Your mandala will be unique, using symbols that are meaningful for you. As a result, I cannot explain exactly how to make your mandala. But I can give guidelines that I hope will be helpful.

Here are the steps I followed in order to make my Personal Mandala, as shown on the preceding page and on the color insert.

I started with a blank piece of paper and a pencil and began by drawing the circumference of a circle onto the paper using a compass. I used a ruler to draw a triangle that was contained within this circle. This created three sections outside the triangle yet still within the circle. In the bottom section, I drew the outline of a phoenix bird. In the right section, I drew the outlines of mountains and aspen trees. In the left section, I drew the outline of a crescent moon in a nighttime sky with stars. I knew that I wanted to make a rainbow of circles radiating out from the initial circle, so I used my colored pencils to indicate this on the paper. Finally, I decided that the whole image needed an additional border of points going around the outermost circumference of beads, so I drew them in, as well. Once I had drawn all these symbols on the piece of paper, I felt ready to draw them on the surface of the leather.

I stretched the leather onto the embroidery hoop, pulling it drum-tight. Using a pair of scissors, I cut out the inner circle that I drew on the paper and traced this circumference onto the leather. (I highly recommend using a pencil for this because you can erase any lines you do not like. If you use a pen, you cannot erase it. Just make sure the pencil eraser is clean, or use a large eraser that is new.) Then I cut the symbols out of the paper and used them as a template to draw the outline of the phoenix, the mountains, and the moon in their respective sections. Once I had these outlines drawn, I began to bead.

I started with the inner circle, using the backstitch. Once I had beaded this portion, I worked on the outlines of the triangle. When I finished these, I followed these lines, making more rows of beads in a triangular shape until I reached the exact central point of the mandala. I had found my center! (Remember this is an internal process as well as external.) Then I worked on each of the three sections until they were completed.

Next, I beaded the rainbow circles in sequence to create the outer circumference of the mandala. I finished by making the points that form the outer boundary of the mandala. The three-dimensional amethyst crystal at the bottom of the triangle was not preplanned; I added it after I had completed the rest of the mandala.

I decided to leave the beadwork in the hoop, allowing the hoop to become the frame for the piece. Then I added some personal touches, such as feathers and charms that held special meaning for me, and hung it on the wall in my studio. After completing my mandala, I investigated the meaning of the symbols I had used in it. If you want to do the same, I have listed books in the Bibliography that you might find useful in interpreting the symbols you choose.

Let me give you some words of reassurance in case you are feeling you are not "creative" enough to do this project. You do not need to be an artist in order to draw the symbols that you want to put into your mandala! You just need to get the basic outlines down so you can bead them. If it gives you any encouragement, I do not draw well at all. Remember, divine inspiration will be working with you once you commit to this process, and the piece will take on a life of its own. I hope you will have the courage to give it a try. Here are some step-by-step guidelines.

Step 1

- On a piece of paper, draw a circle whose diameter is at least ½ inch smaller than the circumference of the embroidery hoop.
- Within this circle, draw the symbols that you feel represent you at your soul level, placing them in whatever configuration feels good to you. You may want to color them in using the colored pencils or crayons.

Step 2

- With a pencil, transfer the outlines of your drawings onto your base material, which has been stretched onto the embroidery hoop. You can cut your symbols out of the paper and use them as patterns to draw the outlines of the symbols onto the base material.

Step 3

- Decide where you want to start beading. You may want to start with the outer circumference of your circle.
- Thread a needle with about 4 feet of thread and prestretch it by pulling it out between your hands, working your way along its entire length.
- Bring the two ends of the thread together so it is doubled. Tie the ends with an overhand knot.
- Cut the tips of thread with scissors and burn them with a lighter or match. (Be careful that the tips do not burn into the knot.)
- Wax the thread so the two threads stick together as one.
- Starting from the back of the base material, bring your needle and thread to the top surface at some point along the circle and pull until the knot is tight against the back.
- Using the backstitch (see figure 1.1 in the Geometric Mandala project on p. 22), begin adding beads along the line you drew

on the front surface, picking up perhaps as many as four beads at a time.

- Continue beading until you have this first circle completed.

Step 4

- Now proceed to bead along the other outlines you drew, progressing to filling inside these outlines as you wish. Use the backstitch to secure your beads as you work.
- If you want to have the beads be more three-dimensional, you can build up layers of beads stitched on top of other beads. You could also include other types of beads, such as pressed-glass flowers and leaves that come up off the flat, two-dimensional plane you are beading on.

Detail, Native American mandala necklace, maker unknown, c. 1990.

- There is no right or wrong way to do this. Just have fun! Watch your symbols as they take on a life of their own. Your choice of beads is just that: your choice! Pick the colors as they feel right to you in each present moment. For instance, if you have chosen a turtle as one of your symbols, maybe it needs to be purple or blue. What colors feel good to you?
- You may want to put a border around the outer circumference of your mandala. As with the Geometric Mandala project, this boundary line will contain and hold the energy within the mandala, keeping its focus on the center. Then again, perhaps you will want to allow the energy in the mandala to project outward; in this case, you probably will not want to bead a boundary around its outer perimeter.
- Be in the flow, and let the piece tell you what it needs (or does not need) in the way of containment.

Step 5: Finishing

- See the suggested finishing options for the Geometric Mandala, step 10 (p. 24). You may also want to attach charms or special accent beads to your finished mandala, which can be stitched on one at a time.

- Once you have decided how you are going to finish it, you may want to make a dangling fringe, as shown in the detail of this Native American mandala necklace. (For fringing techniques, see chapter 2, Project 4, figures 2.9, 2.10, and 2.11.)

Knock on Spirit's Door

Using Beads to Pray

Everyone prays in their own language, and there is no language that God does not understand.

—Duke Ellington

Ancient Connections

We can link beads to early organized religion as far back as neolithic times. By 3000 BCE, people in the Mesopotamian region of eastern Syria mixed beads into the mud for foundation bricks that were used to construct their temples. They would also consecrate the area around their temples by scattering beads throughout the perimeter. It is not hard to imagine this as a symbolic example of using beads to pray for the prosperity of their temples.

In ancient Egypt, beads were an integral part of all aspects of life, including religion. Lois Sherr Dubin writes in *The History of Beads* that the Egyptian word *sha* means "luck" and *sha-sha* means "bead," which suggests that beads were thought to have amuletic or protective properties. The ancient Egyptians were obsessed with religious rituals, and preparing for the afterlife was especially important to them. Beads featured prominently in their burials.

Thousands of beads were often buried with their owners, and on occasion, delicately woven beaded burial shrouds were made to cover the mummified bodies. Perhaps the ancient Egyptian ritual of being buried with beads is not so different from people today who request burial with their beaded rosaries.

Encoded Messages

The English word *bead* comes from two Anglo-Saxon words: *bede,* which means "prayer," and *bidden,* which means "to pray." Encoded in the very word is a relationship between beading and prayer. Many contemporary bead artists mention that when they are beading, they feel as if they are participating in a form of prayer known as meditation. In the catalog that accompanied David Chatt's exhibition, *David Chatt: Two Hands, Twenty Years, and a Billion Beads,* David is quoted as saying, "There is nothing fast or efficient about it. This meditative, painstaking process requires the maker to slow down and to be present for every detail."

As I sit and bead, I also slow down and come fully present. I know that beading requires this meditative frame of mind, and I relish this part of the process. I do most of my beadwork in circular patterns, and the circle is symbolic not only of our physical life but also of our connection to Spirit. Beads themselves are tiny circles, minute mandalas that, when stitched together with consciousness, can become doorways leading to Spirit.

Tribal women in Kenya today sit and bead for hours, often under the umbrella of a shady acacia tree. In the Umoja Uaso Woman's Village, a refuge center for abused Samburu women in northern Kenya, I have observed the women as they bead and have listened to their prayerful songs. Their village is laid out in a circle; they sit and bead on the ground in a circle; their beadwork is circular in shape. Within these circles, they center themselves and, through their beadwork, find hope, peace, and inner joy. Sitting on animal skins with the hard-packed earth beneath them, they sing and pray as they bead.

Beading is communal women's work and one of the only ways they have of earning money to support themselves and their families. Each morning the women bring their completed beaded wares to their open-air curio shop at the edge of the village and carefully place them on display, hoping that tourists will stop to visit the village and make purchases from them. On one of my trips, after watching this daily activity of arranging their beaded items in the curio shop, I learned that no tourists had stopped at the village in over three months. Yet each and every day of those past three months, the women had brought their beadwork to the curio shop with hope in their hearts. For them, the act of beading is an act of hope, a prayer, around which their lives revolve. Beading opens the doorway to Spirit for them and helps them find comfort in an otherwise harsh and often hostile environment. These remote Samburu women understand at a very deep level the connection between beads, beading, and prayer—the encoded meaning of the word *bead.*

Prayer

The word *prayer* comes from the Latin *precarious,* meaning "obtained by begging," and *precari,* meaning "to entreat" or "to ask earnestly, beseech, or implore." Two of the most common forms of prayer are connected to these roots: prayers of *petition,* asking something for ourselves, and prayers of *intercession,* asking something for someone else.

Modern prayer researchers have identified four major categories that cover the wide variety of ways people pray. *Colloquial* prayers are not formal and are offered up in ordinary language. *Petitionary* prayers are prayers in which a person petitions God or Spirit for help or assistance. The third main category of prayer is known as *ritualistic* prayer, when a person prays specific prayers at a prescribed time of day. Muslims, for example, who pray five times a day, saying the same prayers each time, are participating in ritualistic prayers. The fourth major category of prayer is known as *meditation.* There are multiple ways to meditate, most of which involve repetition of a sacred mantra.

There is also a fifth mode of prayer that some have described as a *dialog,* a partnership between the person praying and Spirit based on feelings rather than rote repetition. The key to this form of prayer is that the person praying must *feel* as if her prayer has already been answered in the moment that she is praying. In other words, we have to charge our prayers with emotion in order for them to be effective. Gregg Braden, an internationally renowned pioneer in bridging science and spirituality, describes this lost or hidden form of prayer in his book *Secrets of the Lost Mode of Prayer.* Traveling to Buddhist monasteries in remote Tibet, he discovered monks who used this method of prayer and described it to him with the explanation that feeling *is* the prayer. Healers around the world also appear to understand this aspect of praying and describe it as the fuel behind the healing.

One of the clues as to why this form of prayer works might be found in looking at what quantum physics now refers to by various names, such as the "quantum hologram," the "mind of God," and sometimes simply the "field." Scientists sometimes describe this field as a tightly woven web that makes up the underlying fabric of creation. Native Americans call this the "web of life." Braden describes this field as the "stuff" that lives in the nothing. Whenever we look into the space between us and another person, the presence of the field is there, though we cannot see it with our physical eyes. Rumi, the mystic Sufi poet, understood this field hundreds of years ago when he wrote a poem describing a field out beyond all ideas of wrong-doing and right-doing where we could meet one another. In other words, he was saying that we are all connected by this field of energy.

I have experienced this in a dramatic way when I have entered a Lakota sweat lodge on my hands and knees. It is there that I learned to pray with feeling. The lodge is in the shape of a circle, and the people inside it sit in a circle, connecting us to the other people within the circle and within the sacred circle of life. The ritual begins with the words *Mitakuya Oyasin,* which means "All my Relations," indicating that the participants know that everything is related or interconnected in the great web of life. In the black darkness of the lodge, we return to our Mother Earth's womb, opening to Spirit, releasing old hurts and pains as we pray directly from our hearts. We cry out our prayers with feeling. This kind of praying from the heart is a totally different experience from reciting prayers from a prayer book. Through this form of prayer, we become active cocreators in this web of life or field of energy. And from this perspective, each bead we pick up can become a part of a prayer.

Beads as Part of Religious Practice

Belief systems in every culture in the world, from ancient to modern, incorporate a wide variety of prayer forms. All humans, it seems, have asked and continue to ask for meaning, for guidance, for relief, for blessing. Scholars do not know exactly when or necessarily why beads became part of different religious practices, but they do know that a connection between them has existed for thousands of years. No one knows, either, precisely when or why humans began counting beads as part of their religious practice. Could it simply be due to the fact that beads provide tremendous comfort to the human touch, and when strung together into a circle, they become an easy way for people to keep track of repetitive prayers within their religious tradition? Here again is emphasis on the value of the circle or cycle. Prayers have been recited in cycles since ancient times, and a strand of prayer beads forms a closed circle that is symbolic of cyclical prayer practices.

It is possible that the first example of people using beads to count their prayers can be found in the Hindu faith of ancient India. In her book *Bead One, Pray Too,* religion reporter Kimberly Winston mentions that the first known use of prayer beads dates to a third-century BCE statue of a Hindu holy man draped with beads hung by devotees. Hindu prayer beads are called *malas* and are made from a wide variety of natural materials. They consist of one hundred and eight beads that are used to count breaths or repetitions of the sacred syllables of power called mantras, or for reciting the one hundred and eight names of Brahma, the creator of life. The word *mala* means "rose" or "garland" in Sanskrit.

The adherents of two other world religions that come from India, Sikhism and Jainism, also adopted the practice of using

prayer *malas*. Perhaps this is an indicator of how pervasive the use of counting prayer beads had become to the Indian culture as a whole and helps explain why the practice was assimilated into these newer religions.

Buddhism began in India around 500 BCE and eventually spread throughout Tibet, China, and Japan. There is no documented proof that Siddhartha Gautama, the Indian prince who became the Enlightened One, or the Buddha, used a prayer *mala*, but a legend persists that he encouraged his followers to use them. As Buddhism spread out from the Indian

Carved bone *mala*.

subcontinent, so did the use of the *mala*. Like the Hindu *mala*, the Buddhist *mala* also has 108 beads, or divisions of that number, and can be made from a variety of natural materials, such as stones, human bones, coral, amber, or wood from trees considered sacred, such as the bodhi tree. In Buddhism, the number one hundred and eight corresponds to the number of mental conditions or sinful desires that must be overcome before attaining the perfect state of nirvana.

I am fascinated by Tibetan *malas* that were made from the bones of lamas, Buddhist holy men. The use of human bones was meant to remind a devotee of the Buddhist belief in the transient nature of human existence. According to this belief, nothing is permanent, and everything is in a constant state of change. By using prayer beads made from the bones of a revered teacher, a Buddhist monk was constantly reminded of the lesson on the impermanence of life.

Muslims also use prayer beads, perhaps borrowed from the religious practices of Hindus and Buddhists, though they changed the design to fit their own number symbolism. In Arabic, Muslim prayer beads are called *misbaha* or *subha* and are used as a tool to perform the *dhikr*, a devotional act that focuses on the remembrance of God. There are ninety-nine beads, or subsets of thirty-three, in each *misbaha*, which are used to recite or exalt the ninety-nine attributes of God, according to the teachings of the Prophet Muhammad. By reciting the names of God, Muslims believe they will receive multiple blessings from Allah. *Misbahas* and *subhas* are used after the five set times of daily prayer and at any other times the faithful wish to use them. They are made from many kinds of wood or from natural materials, such as stones, amber, bone, ivory, and coral. Especially revered

Turquoise Buddhist *mala.*

are *misbahas* made from date pits from the Muslim holy cities of Mecca and Medina.

Sufis, who follow an esoteric branch of Islam known as Sufism, use prayer beads known as *tasbih*. They are either made up of three divisions of eleven, equaling thirty-three beads, or have a total count of ninety-nine. Similar to *misbahas*, these prayer beads are also used by Sufi dervishes to recite the ninety-nine attributes of Allah. A Sufi friend of mine explained to me that she uses her *tasbih* to recite the ninety-nine names for Allah and to keep track of the time she devotes to praying. Her *tasbih* contains thirty-three beads made from wood, and she carries it with her at all times in a cloth pouch. These prayer beads are intended only for sacred prayer and are never worn for personal adornment.

Sufi *tasbih.*

Until recently, prayer beads within Christianity had primarily been associated with the Catholic rosary. Scholars speculate that the use of the rosary began in Europe during the Middle Ages as a way for illiterate laity to practice certain Christian prayers. Not able to read Latin, these unschooled people were taught how to use the rosary to keep track of how many psalms they recited. It became the practice to say the "Our Father" (the Lord's Prayer) one hundred and fifty times, so the rosaries were made with the set number of fifty, one hundred, or one hundred and fifty beads that came to be known as Paternoster, Latin for "Our Father." Contemporary Catholic rosaries contain fifty-nine beads divided into five "decades" of ten beads, with four larger beads separating these groups. A short string of five beads hangs down from the circlet of the rosary, culminating in a crucifix at the bottom.

Early Catholic rosaries were made from actual rose petals rolled up to form beads; thus the name "rosary" is derived from the word *rosarium,* or "rose garden." For centuries roses have been associated with the concepts of beauty, perfection, mystery, and love. In Christianity the rose became a symbol for the Virgin Mary and the Christ Child. Modern Catholic rosaries are made from a wide variety of materials that include glass, plastic, wood, clay, shells, semiprecious gemstones, and bone.

Catholic rosary.

Traditionally, members of Protestant denominations have not used prayer beads. However, in the mid 1980s an Episcopalian minister named Rev. Lynn C. Bauman designed an Anglican rosary of thirty-three beads and a cross for his contemplative prayer group. Bauman wanted this new Anglican rosary to be more experimental and free-form than the Catholic rosary, and he encouraged people to experiment and create their own prayers as they used it. The configuration of the Anglican prayer beads relates contemplative prayer use of the rosary to many levels of traditional Christian symbolism. The purpose of these symbols is to help focus and concentrate a person's attention, helping that person attain a deeper level of God-consciousness as she prays. (For instruction on how to make an Anglican rosary, I recommend Kimberly Winston's excellent book *Bead One, Pray Too.*)

If we look within the religious practices of earth-based religions such as Wicca, there are also examples of the use of prayer beads. Many have adopted the Christian discipline and have designed rosaries to fit their own spiritual beliefs and rituals. Their rosaries are made in a wide variety of different sizes, shapes, and colors of beads and often include symbols of personal significance, such as a diversity of pendants, charms, and other decorative elements.

Beads with Spiritual Significance

In many different cultures around the world, people use beads to make objects of deep spiritual significance within their particular society, and the beads often represent their strong beliefs in supernatural forces beyond human control.

People in the regions of Greece, Turkey, and the Middle East have a tradition of using worry beads to ground and calm them when they are stressed or in need of comfort. A strand of worry beads can be made from many different materials, including glass, wood, plastic, amber, semiprecious stones, or clay, and like religious prayer beads, they are tied in the form of a circle. They usually consist of thirty-three beads with a vase-shaped retaining bead ending in a tassel.

Eye beads are another example of beads with spiritual implications—in this case, to protect a person from the evil eye. Scholars think that belief in the evil eye originated as long ago as the Paleolithic era, when people believed—as many still do—in a malevolent force that could bring harm to a person, or even cause death, if they were not protected in some manner from this evil entity. When I traveled to Istanbul in 2007, I saw eye-bead amulets being sold in every bazaar and market. They were mostly made from glass and looked like a big blue eye surrounded by white glass enveloped in a blue matrix. Some of them were key chains meant to be used in a person's automobile, while others were connected to a vertical reproduction of a prayer rug and were meant to hang in a person's home for protection from the evil eye.

Evil eye bead.

All the pastoralist tribes of East Africa use beads for protection from malevolent forces, as well as for personal adornment and as indicators of class, marital status, and age. Lois Sherr

Dubin notes in *The History of Beads* that beads were, and still are, used in Africa to create objects representing spiritual values basic to the survival of the community, and that these objects play a major role in rituals insuring continuity of the group: birth, circumcision, marriage, warriorhood, kingship, and death.

Maasai *olangeshe,* Kenya, 2003. (Photograph by Wendy Ellsworth.)

On one of my trips to Kenya, I was privileged to witness a Maasai *olangeshe,* one of the rituals that warriors participate in to mark the completion of their many years as warriors and their entrance into the next phase of their lives as junior elders. Singing and jumping impossibly high in competitive dancing, the warriors could hardly contain themselves as they gathered for this important ceremony. Each warrior was resplendent, with his head painted with ocher and wearing beaded necklaces and arm and leg bands. Their beaded items had been made for them by their mothers and many girlfriends and were symbolic of their age set and clan. Each bead color holds spiritual significance for the Maasai: red symbolizes blood and the color of the earth where they live, black symbolizes their race, green symbolizes the grass that grows again after the long rains and sustains their cattle and goats, and white symbolizes cow's milk, which they mix with cow's blood and drink as a way of surviving in their harsh climate.

In northern Kenya, every Samburu child is given a protective amulet to wear around his or her neck at birth. This might be a specific colored bead or a leather pouch containing assorted talismanic substances. Strings of colored beads or ostrich eggshell beads may be tied around the child's waist for added protection against malevolent forces. Cowrie shells are particularly prized for their spiritual significance. When Samburu women clothe themselves for traditional prayers, they must always include cowrie shell beads as part of their attire. Cowrie shells are treasured as such good-luck charms that they will be recycled over and over again and never thrown away.

On their beaded headdresses, Samburu women wear a metal pendant that hangs down on their fore-heads. There is some controversy as to the meaning of this pendant, with some scholars believing that it is a fertility symbol. However, in talking with Rhodia Mann, an expert on Samburu culture who lives in Nairobi, I discovered another possible explanation for its spiritual significance to Samburu women. According to her research, she has been led to believe that this symbol is meant to be a reminder to the women of their mytho-logical descent from the planet Venus, and thus it has tremendous spiritual significance and value in their lives. At the very least, every Samburu woman wears one of these pendants as part of her beaded regalia, along with hundreds of strands of colorful beads and multiple beaded circular collars, earrings, and beaded armbands. Similar to the Maasai, each bead color also has deep spiritual significance for the Samburu. They pray as they bead, singing to Ng'ai (their name for God) while they offer up prayers for good rains, fertile cows, healthy children, and enough food to eat.

Samburu woman with star pendant, Umoja Oaso Woman's Village, Kenya, 2004. (Photograph by Wendy Ellsworth.)

Samburu woman with star pendant, Umoja Oaso Woman's Village, Kenya, 2004. (Photograph by Wendy Ellsworth.)

Creating Prayer Beads

While the number and arrangement of beads—along with their color, size, and materials—vary from culture to culture, what most of these people who use beads as spiritual objects have in common (with the exception of Buddhists) is a belief in a Higher Power, with whom they can communicate through prayer. Their prayer beads are a vital link to the spiritual realm or to the divine source of all life.

I was raised in a faith tradition that did not use prayer beads. While I occasionally observed from a distance devout Catholics praying their rosaries, I was not really exposed to prayer beads until much later in life. For me, the very act of beading became my prayer practice, with each bead symbolizing a prayer mandala on its own. My beaded SeaForms glorify the beauty of underwater coral sea life and are a prayer for its survival in today's global warming climate changes. My beaded jewelry extols the beauty of Mother Nature in all her glorious colors and seasonal wardrobes. Beading is a meditative, spiritual practice for me, and I cherish the time I can sit and bead in order to create a piece of bead art that is unique and spiritually fulfilling.

Glass Heart Pendant, Susan Strong, 1½ x ¾ inches, lampworked Italian medium amber colored crystal, 22k gold fused to surface, *Ping's Ashes,* 2008. (Photograph by Susan Strong.)

On a smaller scale, I enjoy making beaded prayer pouches that I fill with objects that have special meaning to me. These might be made by stitching beads onto pieces of leather that become a medicine amulet pouch, or might be made entirely of beads stitched to one another using various bead-weaving techniques. I also occasionally enjoy stringing up prayer beads for friends who are in a period of life crisis. As I add on each bead, I send prayers of love and light to them, asking only that whatever is in their highest and best good be manifested in their life.

Another bead artist, Susan Strong, creates heart-shaped pendants using hot glass into which she mixes the cremated ashes of friends or family members who have died. When she gives them to relatives of the deceased to be worn in memory of their loved one, these sacred glass hearts bring the wearer a sense of peace. Susan's work has grown into making complete beaded neckpieces that include the heart-shaped pendants along with other beads, often in the favorite colors of the deceased and perhaps their birthstones, as well. She treats this work with utmost respect. It has become a meditative practice that is closely linked to her spiritual journey, and she prays for guidance in each step of the process as she creates her own form of "prayer" beads.

In *A String and a Prayer,* beaders Eleanor Wiley and Maggie Oman Shannon offer excellent advice on the value of creating your own strand of prayer beads. The very act of weaving beads together can be a spiritual act and a means of connecting with the Divine. As you string the beads together and infuse them with your prayers and creative intention, you will be giving them your soul energy. This becomes beading for the soul, something Susan Strong understands well.

I will give directions for making two projects that involve using beads in a prayerful manner. The first project is a strand of Personal Prayer Beads that you can tailor to your own individual prayer practice and is geared toward novice beaders. The second one, a prayer pouch made with Japanese seed beads, involves two different bead-weaving techniques: the ladder stitch and the brick stitch. The exercise "Blessing the Materials" can be done before starting either project, and the meditation "Accessing Your Right-Brain Creative Spirit" is especially good for Project 3, Personal Prayer Beads. It can also be used any time you feel the urge to tap into your creative energy source.

Before you begin this project (or any of the projects in the book), I recommend this exercise to bless the materials you will be using. It will help bring you into a more contemplative frame of mind as you begin to work.

EXERCISE
Blessing the Materials

1. For this ritual, you will need either some form of smudge or an incense wand and matches or a lighter.
2. If you are smudging, you can make smudge from dried sage, sweetgrass, or the needles of the arborvitae tree, or you can find smudging wands commercially available. You will also

Abalone shell with sage smudge stick.

need a container in which to burn the smudge, such as a large shell or ceramic pot, and a bird feather large enough to blow the smoke over your materials.

3. Gather the materials for making your prayer pouch (or other project) and whatever form of smudge or incense you have chosen to use. Have them on a table in front of where you are sitting.

4. Sit quietly and take three deep breaths, releasing as much tension with the out breath as you can. Relax your shoulders, your facial muscles, and your jaw.

5. Bring your attention to your breath and into the "now" of this moment.

6. When the time feels right, ask for help from Spirit in this blessing ritual you are about to begin.

7. Open your eyes and look at the prayer pouch materials that are in front of you.

8. Notice the colors, shapes, and sizes of the beads you have chosen for your project.

9. Notice how you feel when you look at them. Allow their colors to penetrate your energy field, and notice how and where they affect you internally, if at all. Do they have something to say to you? Ask them—and listen for an answer.

10. When this process feels complete, you may go on to the next step.

11. Light the incense wand or smudge.

12. Ask the Spirit of the substance being burned to actively assist you in blessing your materials. (Even though this substance is no longer "alive," it still has an energy that resides within it.)

13. If using an incense stick, gently wave the smoking stick over the materials for your prayer pouch, blessing them with the smoke. Silently state your intention for this ritual and why you have chosen to make this prayer pouch. This could take

the form of a prayer in which you invoke the blessing of one of your angels, the Creative Spirit, or your Higher Self.

14. If burning smudge, use the feather to gently waft the smoke over the materials, as above.

15. When you have blessed all the materials, be sure to extinguish the smudge or incense, or place the incense stick into an incense stand to continue burning safely.

Before you begin project 3, you might want to sit quietly and pray for guidance and direction. I have provided a meditation to help you move into a more contemplative state of being. Also, remember that your feelings are the fuel for your prayers, so pay attention to how you are feeling in the present moment of making your beaded creation. You may want to keep a beading journal beside you to write down any specific feelings and/or thoughts that come up while you work.

MEDITATION
Accessing Your Right-Brain Creative Spirit

1. You may choose to light a candle or incense and turn on a water fountain, if you happen to have one available.

2. Sit comfortably in a chair with your feet on the floor and your back straight.

3. Gently close your eyes.

4. Bring yourself into the present moment and take three deep breaths.

5. Watch each breath come in and go out, consciously observing each inhalation and exhalation.

6. Continue to breathe consciously. With each exhalation, allow the tension in your body to begin to release.

7. Set your responsibilities and duties aside for now; you can return to them later.

8. Gently ask the chatter of your left-brain "monkey mind" to calm down so you can come more fully present into this moment now.

9. Relax your jaw, your brow, your shoulders, all places where you hold tension in your body.

10. Notice if there are any other places you are holding tension; breathe into them consciously in order to release this tightness. Feel yourself lightening up.

11. Can you smell the incense or candle you lit?

12. Can you hear the water trickling in the fountain?

13. Can you hear the wind blowing through the trees outside?

14. Just concentrate on observing your breath coming in and going out, in and out. You have nowhere to go and nothing to do in this moment, now, other than give yourself permission to be the observer of your breath. When other thoughts come up, gently release them and come back to watching your breath.

15. If you want to focus on a mantra, try repeating, "Be still and know that I am God."

16. Can you feel a new sense of inner peace and calmness? If so, allow the Presence of this feeling of peace to just *be*. Sit and be present with it for a few moments. You may notice that there is also a feeling of joy associated with this place of peace. Breathe into this sense of joy, and bring Presence to it, as well.

17. Perhaps you will notice a color that will come to you. Focus on this color and allow it to fill you up with its radiance.

18. If you want, set your intention for the beading you are about to work on. Ask for help from Spirit to guide you.

19. Silently invite your wondrous "inner child" to come out and play with you as you work. She will be more than happy to stimulate your creative juices and dance with you. Think of the adjectives that apply to her: happy, joyful, spontaneous, imaginative, flexible, playful, inquisitive, curious, creative.

20. When you are ready, open your eyes and notice how you are feeling, right now, in this moment. Do you feel a difference from when you began this meditation? Are you feeling more centered and more balanced?

21. As you create this project, let each bead and every stitch be a prayer of gratitude for the many blessings in your life. Let the love in your heart radiate out through your hands and into the pouch as you bead in the Creative Spirit.

Personal Prayer Beads

Each strand of Personal Prayer Beads that you make will be unique. You can choose your own palette of colors, sizes, texture, and shapes of beads, and decide whether you want to use random or repetitive patterns within the strand. You may decide to add various amulets, animal totems, or glass, ceramic, stone, or gemstone beads. I will give some basic directions for a continuous strand of beads that will become a necklace, but if you want to make a bracelet or handheld prayer piece, you can adapt the directions accordingly. Experiment and have fun!

Prayer Beads for Barack Obama, Wendy Ellsworth, 2008. (For a color photo of this project, see color plate 3a.)

As you gather your materials, focus your thoughts on the person for whom you are making these prayer beads. Hold the image of that person in your mind and heart and ask for guidance in selecting the beads for his or her gift. Because there is no right or wrong way to do this project, you will need to trust that whatever you choose will be perfect for this prayer strand. As you work, offer up each bead as a prayer. This energy will go into what you are making and will help transform what would otherwise be just a piece of jewelry into an object imbued with soul and Spirit.

MATERIALS

- Beads: The choice of beads is entirely up to you! Anything with a hole can be considered a bead. Check your local bead store for new beads or thrift stores for old jewelry that can be taken apart. Glass, stone, ceramic, gemstone, paper, wood, seeds, shells, and metal are all possibilities. You may want to include a large focal bead in the center of the piece. You might also choose to add amulets, animal totem beads, and silk tassels.

- Stringing material: Your choice of stringing material will be determined by the sizes of the holes in the beads you choose to use and the overall weight of the finished product. Synthetic sinew works well and makes it easy to string the beads, as well as tie off in the center of the back. You could also use raffia, Soft Flex, or Beadalon wire. (If you use wire, you will need the correct size of crimp beads and the crimping tool to flatten them, along with wire cutters.)

Handheld prayer beads, Wendy Ellsworth, 2009.

- Scissors
- Beading mat
- Ott light or desk lamp

STEP 1

- Pull approximately 40 inches of sinew (or whatever stringing material you have chosen) off the spool.
- You do not need to cut it unless you would rather start adding beads in the center of the necklace, working up both sides. If you do cut it, place an overhand knot at one end so the beads will not fall off the end.

STEP 2

- Pick up the beads you have chosen to work with and add them one at a time onto the sinew, pushing them all the way to the spool or to the knot.
- Let each bead be a prayer as you add it one by one.

STEP 3

- Decide where the center of the necklace will be on your length of sinew, as this will be where you string on your focal bead. (On my *Prayer Beads for Barack Obama,* I tied the large silver cylinder with two knots to secure it before continuing to add beads.)

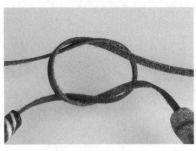

Square knot.

Step 4

• When you have added all the beads onto the sinew that you want to include, cut the sinew from the spool, leaving at least a 3-inch length at both ends to tie off.

Step 5

• Tie the ends of the sinew in a square knot (right over left, pull and tighten, then left over right and tighten).

• Pass the ends back through several beads on each side of the necklace before cutting off.

Beaded Prayer Pouch

This small Beaded Prayer Pouch is made using two bead-weaving stitches known as the ladder and the brick stitch. You begin with the ladder stitch, which forms the base row, and off of this base row you begin working in two-bead brick stitch. The project works up quickly because you are using two beads in each stitch. You can use a main bead color with a second contrasting accent color for the edges of the flap, and you can incorporate a wide variety of interesting and fun beads in the bottom fringe. The strap is a single strand of strung beads in which you can include some of the same beads used in the bottom fringe.

MATERIALS

- Japanese seed beads, size 11, in two colors: color 1, 20 grams; color 2, 10 grams
- Miscellaneous beads for fringe and strap
- Cube bead, 4 millimeter, for clasp (or clasp of your choice)
- Silamide thread size A or Nymo size B to match bead color 1
- Sharps short beading needles, size 12
- Synthetic wax
- Scissors: small with sharp point
- Beading mat
- Ott light or desk lamp

Beaded Prayer Pouch, Wendy Ellsworth, 2008. (For a color photograph of this project, see color plate 2a.)

PROJECT PREPARATION

- To start, pull off approximately 9 feet of thread and pre-stretch it by pulling it out between your hands, working your way along its entire length.
- Thread a needle. You will work the thread single width, leaving half the length as a tail that will be used for the fringe at the bottom edge.

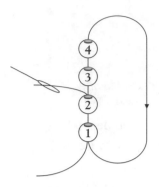

2.1. Ladder stitch, step 1.

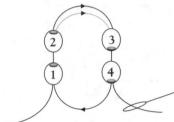

2.2. Ladder stitch, step 2.

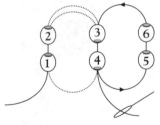

2.3. Ladder stitch, step 3.

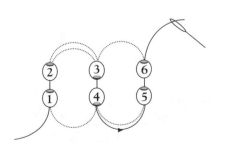

2.4. Ladder stitch, step 4.

Base Row: *Ladder Stitch*

- You will be making a two-bead ladder, thirty-six units in length.
- There are five steps to getting the ladder stitch going.

STEP 1

(see figure 2.1)

- Pick up four beads and run them down to the end of your thread, leaving a tail that is approximately 4 feet in length.
- Pass back through beads 1 and 2 again, in the same direction as you put them onto the thread. (When you do this, beads 3 and 4 will lie side by side with beads 1 and 2, as shown in figure 2.2.)

STEP 2

(see figure 2.2)

- Stitch down into beads 3 and 4.

STEP 3

(see figure 2.3)

- Pick up two more beads (5 and 6), and pass the needle down through the previous two beads (3 and 4).

STEP 4

(see figure 2.4)

- Stitch up into beads 5 and 6.

STEP 5

(see figure 2.5)

- Pick up two more beads (7 and 8), and pass the needle up through the previous two beads (5 and 6), then back down through beads 7 and 8. Figure 2.5 shows the next two beads (9 and 10) on the needle ready to stitch down into 7 and 8.

COMPLETING THE ROW

- Continue to repeat steps 3, 4, and 5 until your total count is thirty-six units of two beads in length. (Notice that the steps rotate, starting either from the bottom or the top of the stitch just completed.)

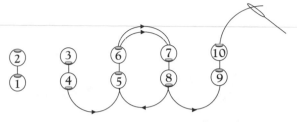

2.5. Ladder stitch, step 5.

- Join ends of ladder to make a circle. Stitch up, down, and up again so your working thread is coming out of the top, and the tail is coming out of bottom of ladder row.
- Note: you can increase or decrease this base row, but keep an even count.

Row 2: Two-Bead Tubular Brick Stitch

- You will be using a two-bead brick stitch in color 1, working your way around the base row until you come back to your first stitch. You will then connect the final stitch in this row to the first stitch, so you will be working in tubular two-bead brick stitch.

Detail of joining ends of ladder to make circle.

STEP 1

- To start, pick up two beads (1 and 2 in the first diagram in figure 2.6); pass the needle from *back to front* under the thread that connects the *first* two units in the bead ladder.

STEP 2

- Stitch from *bottom to top* through beads 2 and 1 again. The first brick stitch is now complete.
- Repeat these two steps along the entire length of the bead ladder base, moving over to the next thread from the two-bead ladder base for each stitch. The middle diagram in figure 2.6 shows the next two beads (3 and 4) on the needle ready for step 1. You will stitch from back to front between the

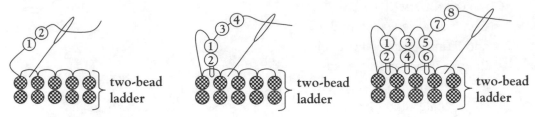

2.6. Two-bead brick stitch.

second and third units in the bead ladder, underneath the thread that connects them, and from bottom to top through beads 4 and 3. The third diagram in figure 2.6 shows the first three stitches in place and the next two beads (7 and 8) on the needle ready to take step 1 in stitch 4. You will stitch from back to front between the fourth and fifth units in the bead ladder, underneath the thread that connects them, and bottom to top through beads 8 and 7.

Completing the Row

- You are now ready to connect the last stitch in the row to the first stitch. (You will do this at the end of each row.) To do this, after completing the final stitch in the row, pass the needle *down* through the two beads of the first stitch, then back *up* through the two beads of the last stitch. You are now in position to begin the next row of two-bead brick stitch.

Rows 3–10

- Work in two-bead tubular brick stitch, repeating directions for row 2.

Row 11

- Work eighteen stitches in one-bead tubular brick stitch. To do this, pick up a single bead instead of two beads. For contrast, use color 2 for the first and last bead in the row. At the end of this short row, you will reverse direction to begin making the flap.

Row 12: Making the Flap
(decreasing in one-bead flat brick stitch)

STEP 1
- Pick up two beads. Pass the needle from front to back underneath the *second* thread from the edge in the previous row. (Bead 1 can be color 2.) (See figure 2.7.)

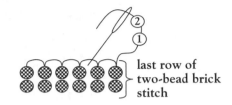

last row of two-bead brick stitch

2.7. Decreasing in single-bead flat brick stitch, step 1.

STEP 2
- Stitch from *bottom to top* through bead 2, *down* through bead 1, and *up* through bead 2 again. (See figure 2.8.)

STEP 3
- Pick up bead 3. Pass the needle under the third thread from the edge from *back to front*. (For each stitch, you will move over one thread along the top edge.)

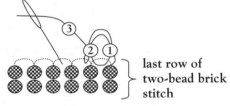

last row of two-bead brick stitch

2.8. Decreasing in single-bead flat brick stitch, step 2.

STEP 4
- Stitch from *bottom to top* back through bead just added (3).
- Repeat steps 3 and 4 across this row for a total of seventeen beads.

Rows 13–27
- Following the directions for row 12, continue working back and forth across each previous row, decreasing one stitch each row until you have a final stitch of two beads. (Each row will have a natural decrease of a single bead.)
- Do not cut the thread. You will use this thread for the clasp loop.

Clasp
(see color plate 3b)
- Attach a 4-millimeter cube bead (or clasp of choice) to the second row of the pouch on the front. (Fold the flap over the front. and it will indicate exactly where this clasp needs to be placed.)

- To do this, start a new thread so that it comes out the top of the ninth two-bead stitch from the left edge of the pouch.
- Pick up two seed beads, one cube bead, one seed bead.
- Pass back through the cube bead and two seed beads.
- Stitch down into the tenth two-bead stitch from the left edge.
- Go through all the beads used in the clasp a second time to reinforce the clasp.
- Do not end the thread. (You will use it to close up the pouch at the bottom edge.)

Loop
(see color plate 2b)

- Using the thread coming out of the final stitch of the flap, add on enough seed beads to make a small loop that will fit over the clasp beads.
- Stitch into the second bead of the final row and pass back through the loop beads again to reinforce.
- End the thread.

Bottom Edge of Pouch

- To stitch the bottom edge of the pouch closed, use the leftover thread from adding the clasp.
- Weave it down to the bottom edge so it exits one of the beads along the bottom edge.
- Stitch the two sides of the pouch together by passing the needle under the edge threads from side to side.
- Work your way from one side to the other until the entire bottom edge is closed up.
- If you still have plenty of thread, you can use it for some of the bottom fringe. If not, end the thread.

Fringe

- Add the needle to the original tail.
- Make a fringe that comes out of every bead along the entire bottom edge of the pouch. It can be as long as you want and can include as many interesting beads as you are inspired to

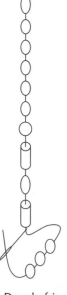

2.9. Dangle fringe.

use! Figures 2.9, 2.10, and 2.11 are examples of types of fringe you may want to make. Figure 2.9 shows a simple dangle fringe. Figure 2.10 shows one form of beaded leaf fringe that you might use at the bottom of a dangle fringe. Figure 2.11 shows a second form of beaded leaf fringe where the fringe has leaves coming off its sides.

- End the thread. (You may need to add on thread to complete fringe)

2.10. Leaf fringe 1.

Strap

(see color plate 2b)

- Pull off approximately 36 inches of thread and prestretch.
- Add the needle and bring to the middle of the thread to work doubled.
- Attach the thread to the pouch so it exits the two-bead stitch at the top right of the pouch, just beside the first bead of the decrease row of the flap.
- String beads onto the thread in the pattern of your choice until the strap is long enough to be able to attach to the pouch and still fit around your head.
- Attach the end of this strap to the opposite side of the pouch, making sure it fits around your head before securing.
- End the thread.

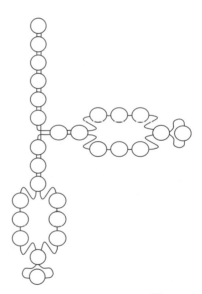

2.11. Leaf fringe 2.

WEARING YOUR BEADED PRAYER POUCH

Place any items inside your pouch that feel right to you. You might choose to write out a prayer on a small piece of paper, fold it, and put it inside your pouch. Or you might want to place a small photo of a loved one inside. Remember that your prayer pouch was made with love and will continue to radiate this love out into the world as you wear it.

Stir the Pot

In Search of the Authentic Self

Don't Push the River
(it flows by itself)

—Barry Stevens

Be Here Now!

In 1989, I began a new body of work that became my Beaded Stick Figure series. Walking through my eastern Pennsylvania forest one day, I noticed a tree branch on the ground, and when I picked it up, it spoke to me: "Bead me!" I found that rather amusing and brought the stick into my studio to study it and think about its request to be beaded. The branch resembled a human torso with arms but no legs, and as I studied it, I began to see the potential for transforming it into a beaded figure that could be mounted on a base of wood.

I started by beading around the surface of the stick using the gourd stitch. I used this bead-weaving technique to completely cover the stick with seed beads, and the stick became a fragile wooden armature for the woven beads. I used the colors of the chakras to indicate the different parts of the stick's "body," starting

Psyche, Wendy Ellsworth, 15 x 9 x 7 inches, glass seed beads, wooden stick, feather, wooden base, 1989.

with red beads for the Root chakra and ending with violet beads for the seventh chakra at the top of the figure. (I will say much more about chakra colors in chapter 4.) I partially beaded the "arms" and placed a feather in the "hand" of one arm. Securing the three-dimensional figure onto a wooden base, I was excited to complete my first sculptural beaded form. I titled the piece *Psyche,* which turned out to be most prophetic.

Little did I know that I was about to plumb the depths of my psyche and bring to the surface parts of myself that need to be examined, processed, healed, and transformed. I was about to discover how beading can "stir the pot" and lead to a deeper understanding of the self. Beading was about to become a conscious therapeutic process for me, a safe way to process and heal some very painful memories.

I began to look for other tree branches that resembled the human body in some way, bringing them into my studio to study them and consider how I might turn them into beaded sculptural forms. I titled my second beaded stick figure *Black Orpheus.* When my memories of childhood molestation began surfacing, I understood that I had been violated, betrayed, and abandoned, and I could see how these wounds had set up a lifetime of feeling unworthy. I found that I could use each stick figure to explore hidden aspects of my psyche, and the beaded sticks became tools to process my fury, my grief, and my loss of innocence, to transform my old wounds into positive, creative acts. I entered a "dark night of the soul" and was determined not only to work through my anguish but also to emerge at the other end as a new, revitalized woman. In my beadwork I found comfort, strength, courage, and solace while I processed through this life crisis.

Making *Black Orpheus* was pivotal for my inner healing. As I beaded the image, I allowed myself to feel anything and everything that my body needed. Every single bead became an emotion that I needed to express through the creative process of bead weaving.

The image I created looked satanic, almost gleeful in its dance of perverted sexuality. Molesting children is an act of heinous cruelty almost beyond comprehension, and I needed to transform my grief and reweave my shattered web of life. I needed to reclaim my sense of self-worth, to open to my true emotions, reconnect with my sensuality and sexuality, and restore healthy boundaries.

Beading became my sanity, and shining a light into the dark recesses of my psyche became an exciting journey of self-discovery. Because beading demanded that I be fully present to the process, it helped me give birth to a new self that was able to trust and love again. Beading is a wonderful teacher of *Be Here Now*, the spiritual philosophy taught by mentors such as Ram Dass in his book of the same name and spiritual teacher and author Eckart Tolle in *The Power of Now.* According to this philosophy, there is only this present moment, the *now*. The past has already come and gone, and the future has not arrived yet. It is in the ever-present *now* that we can find the true self. Surrendering to what is happening in the present moment is part of saying *yes* to what *is*. Surrender is not a passive state or action but a process of yielding to what is happening in the moment. It is an act of accepting the moment unconditionally and knowing that, at a higher level, there is meaning and purpose in this moment, now. By giving up resistance to what *is*, we enter into the flow of life.

Black Orpheus, Wendy Ellsworth, 17 x 9 x 7 inches, glass seed beads, wooden stick with pine cone, wooden base, 1990.

This time of beading helped me pave the way to a new level of authenticity and wholeness. I knew how much I had healed when the next beaded stick figure I made after *Black Orpheus* was a female form that I titled *Pink Stockings.* The stick was definitely a female image with open legs and a vulva showing in her "crotch." I wove beaded stockings around the legs of the stick, using pink beads, and displayed it lying on a small stone under its torso for support.

Masks of the False Self

Resisting the Mirror is a stick figure I made portraying the contortions we go through when the mirror of truth is presented to us and we resist looking into it out of fear of what will be reflected there. It is not easy to admit to our ugly side, to those emotions, thoughts, and deeds that are less than honorable or nice. Many of us, myself included, would rather go into denial when that mirror gets held up and someone says to us, "You need to take a look!" Denial of the truth can be agonizing when we refuse to own up to how we have misbehaved or mistreated another person.

Resisting the Mirror,
Wendy Ellsworth, glass
seed beads, wooden
stick, slate base, 1994.
(Photograph by George
Erml.)

However, if we have the courage and take the challenge of looking into the mirror when it is held up for us, we will likely encounter a mask of the "false self" looking back at us. Perhaps we have presented this masked self to the world for a long time, hoping that we will be accepted and feel safe, and we have eventually come to believe in the illusion that our masked selves represent who we truly are. We may have forgotten that we are spiritual beings having a human experience, not humans trying to "get spiritual." Spirituality is not outside of us; it is at the core of our true self.

Masks of the false self are an illusion that keeps us from knowing our true self. The mask gets activated when we deny our feelings of fear, pride, or hate, and it represents an unconscious desire to avoid these unpleasant feelings. We may create many masks, each one like a shell covering up our true essence, and we end up presenting an image of ourselves to the world based on who we think we *should* be, or who we think our family, culture, or society *expects* us to be.

We all have masks that formed in our childhood years, masks that helped us escape the hurts and feelings of shame we suffered, or that protected us from seeing the lies, deceit, and forms of betrayal we experienced by those in positions of power over us. We also have masks that form in adulthood as we continue to "resist the mirror" of our true selves, refusing to accept responsibility for those parts of ourselves that we believe are less than holy. Letting go of these "false" selves that no longer serve us can be a way of lightening our load and helping us become more authentic in our search for wholeness.

There are several bead artists who have been exploring masks of the false self through their beadwork. Joyce J. Scott is a master seed bead artist who is fearless in portraying not only personal masks but also cultural and societal masks through her artwork. While she uses humor to get at the core of her message, most of her pieces explore topics that smack us right in the gut. Racial prejudice, sexism, rape, the myth of the black male's sexual prowess, and the role of black mammies in white racist families are all masks she has examined and worked into her bead art. She also addresses the "taboo" topic of violence, from race-related riots to sexual abuse, with biting humor, as evidenced in her piece titled *Head Shot*. In an article titled "All About Joyce," award-winning journalist Lee Lawrence wrote that she portrays violence in jewelry not to glorify or dismiss it, but to lure people closer until they realize they are looking at a mirror of the violence within themselves.

Head Shot, Joyce J. Scott, 18½ x 4½ x 4½ inches, glass seed beads, thread, glass, bullets, 2008. (Photograph by Michael Koryta.)

Joyce's work holds up a mirror that shows us the many masks of our social stereotypes, masks that for many of us elicit an uncomfortable response because of the truth we see reflected there. As an African American woman, Joyce has personally experienced the effects of segregation and legalized discrimination—what Lawrence described in his article as the "cruel underbelly of humanity." But you will not find a more upbeat, inspiring, and creative person in the crafted arts today. She wants the viewer to wake up and become more aware of the personal masks, stereotypes, and prejudices that we all hold in our psyches, and she is using her beadwork to achieve this goal.

Bead artist NanC Meinhardt's mask series is another example of beads being used to explore the false self. NanC spent fifteen months creating five masks in her seminal Let Me In, Let Me Out mask series. She chose the mask format as a means of expressing the different adaptations the members of a mythical family might adopt in their search for individuality and self-identity. She beaded each mask over a wooden armature in her signature free-form right-angle weave stitch. A therapist by training, NanC uses her beadwork to look within herself and examine her thoughts and emotions, expressing them outwardly through her bead art.

Mother Load, NanC Meinhardt, 12 x 8 x 4 inches, seed beads, 22-karat gold vintage seed beads, pressed glass beads, freshwater pearls, silk cord, nylon thread, wooden armature, 1996. (Photograph by Tom Van Eynde.)

One piece in this series, titled *Mother Load,* portrays the heaviness and weight that the archetypal mask of the Mother carries. All of us who wear the mask of the Mother can relate to the title of NanC's piece, as well as to the burdens that go along with it. Motherhood can appear glamorous, but the day-to-day realities of being Mother can also be overwhelming and stultifying, causing us to deny the feelings of rage and angst that go along with the Mother mask in order to appear as the "good" mother.

Similar to Joyce J. Scott's seminal work, NanC's masks draw us in with their beauty, opening a door to a deeper level of ourselves as we ponder their meaning and relevance in our own lives. Each time we dare to look into the mirror and uncover hidden aspects of our true selves, we come closer to being able to be our authentic selves, unmasked and real.

The inspiration of these two dynamic bead artists challenges us to use beading as a means of "stirring the pot" and examining what comes floating up to the surface of our consciousness. As we work to portray these hidden aspects of our psyches through our beading, we can bring the masks of our false selves into the light, where they can be transformed. Beading in this way becomes a therapeutic process, a tool for personal metamorphosis.

Archetypes

Many of our masks are archetypal. The term *archetype* was coined by the Swiss psychiatrist Carl Jung early in the twentieth century. According to Jung, there are visual symbols or energetic imprints that exist in every person's psyche that he termed "archetypes": unconscious patterns of behavior that represent a compilation of collective human experiences reaching back into prehistory that provide deep structure for human motivation and meaning.

Dustin Wedekind, *Ungud (Snake Goddess)*, 6 x 3 x 3 inches, beads, sequins, thread, glue, vinyl tubing, plastic action figure, 2006. (Photograph by Dustin Wedekind.)

In *The Hero with a Thousand Faces*, mythologist Joseph Campbell identified the archetype of the "Hero," and the quest that the Hero undertakes. This archetype portrays a psychological as well as spiritual journey inside of ourselves that often involves a "death" and a "resurrection" into a higher level of consciousness. Campbell followed the Hero's journey through many of the folk tales and myths of the world, a rich source of material for understanding archetypal behavior.

In 2000, the Japanese manufacturers of Miyuki Delica beads sponsored their second international challenge, and they chose as their theme "Myths and Folk Tales." Bead artists from around the globe submitted their entries, and eighty-seven of them were published in a colorful booklet titled *Myths & Folk Tales: Selections from the 2nd International Miyuki Delica Challenge.* Joseph Campbell would have been delighted with these fabulous pieces. Each one portrays the artist's imaginative rendition of a particular myth or folk tale in two or three dimensions. Carol Wilcox Wells wrote in her judge's comments that she was humbled by the creativity of the artists and by the time spent designing, planning, and executing these thematic works of art, which she felt took great courage to create. I would agree. Turning an archetype, a myth, or a folk tale into a concrete object requires a willingness to say "Yes!" to the challenge of looking deeply within our psyche and giving personal meaning to what we have chosen to portray.

Phoenix, Wendy Ellsworth, 6-inch diameter, glass seed beads, leather, 1982.

When I was making beaded leather handbags, I sometimes used mythological images as the central beaded motif. The phoenix bird was a subject I especially enjoyed beading, with its beautiful feathers cascading over its colorful body. The symbolism of the phoenix rising from the ashes speaks deeply to my soul: when we go into the darkness to do our inner work, there is always the promise that we will be reborn from the ashes of the fires we have walked through, reemerging into the light, ready to fly again.

I was once commissioned to make a large leather handbag with the beaded image of a Sankofa bird on the front. Originating in Ghana, West Africa, Sankofa is a mythical bird whose head is turned so it is looking over its back. It symbolizes the action of looking backward to understand the past in order to move forward to build the future. Implied in its symbolism is the value of looking inward in order to gain the necessary wisdom for the future.

Quetzalcoatl, the plumed serpent god of the Mayans and Aztecs, is another mythological bird image that I have been inspired to recreate. I spent two winters making a ceremonial "button robe," similar in concept to the magnificent button robes of the Pacific Northwest coastal tribes, the Tlingit, Haida, and Kwagiutl.

These native peoples began to make magnificent ceremonial robes in the mid-1800s using blankets brought to them as trade items by the Hudson Bay Company. They used mother-of-pearl buttons to outline their family crests (indicators of each person's rank, hereditary rights, and obligations) on fabric appliquéd onto the blankets. These crests depicted various animals such as bear, killer whale, and beaver, as well as other legendary creatures, such as Sisiutl the two-headed serpent. Each family owns its own crest, which is passed down through a matrilineal heritage.

I wanted to make a similar garment and decided to depict Quetzalcoatl as my central motif. Like the symbol of the phoenix, Quetzalcoatl also symbolizes death and resurrection. I stitched 1,554 mother-of-pearl buttons I inherited from my paternal grandmother to red wool appliquéd onto a black wool blanket to make the robe.

An important archetype for women is the "Wild Woman." Poet, psychoanalyst, and posttrauma specialist Clarissa Pinkola Estés delineates this archetype in her remarkable book *Women Who Run with the Wolves: Myths and Stories of the Wild Woman Archetype,* in which she describes the Wild Woman archetype as

the source of the feminine, the innate instinctual self. According to Estés, Wild Woman is the patroness of all creative people—painters, writers, sculptors, dancers, even bead artists—because Wild Woman's main occupation is with the work of invention. Wild Woman resides in our guts where our intuition and instinct dwell, not in our heads. We know Wild Woman through our feelings, not through our intellect. Estés tells us that our Wild Woman archetype is completely essential to our mental health and to the health of our souls.

Quetzalcoatal Button Robe,
Wendy Ellsworth, 60 x 66 inches,
mother-of-pearl buttons,
wool, wool blanket, 1993.

Doing soul work through the craft of beading is a perfect method of tapping into our Wild Woman archetype. After reading *Women Who Run with the Wolves: Myths and Stories of the Wild Woman Archetype,* I made a series of Wild Woman handbags from soft doeskin leather, cylindrical in shape, with leather fringe skirts and snakeskin crotches. I included beaded designs stitched directly to the body of the purse, along with buttons, shells, freshwater pearls, silver conchas, and anything else that I was moved to embellish on the surface of the bag.

Wild Woman Purse, Wendy Ellsworth, 9 x 6 x 6 inches, glass seed beads, freshwater pearls, mother-of-pearl buttons, snake skin, leather, silver conchas, 1993.

Shaman's Bag, Wendy Ellsworth, 9 x 6 x 6 inches, glass seed beads, Biggs Jasper, silver conchas, bone buttons, dentalium shells, fused glass eye, bison leather, suede, 2000.

I made a final piece in the Wild Woman Handbag series that I titled *Shaman's Bag*. The design includes beaded images of eagle, bear, butterfly, dragonfly, owl, weasel, dolphin, a 360-degree rainbow, and a smoking medicine pipe. A large cabochon of Biggs Jasper is highlighted by a beaded bezel of seed beads, entwined by the smoke coming out of the medicine pipe. I stitched silver conchas and bone buttons with the imprint of a wolf's paw embedded in them around the top of the bag.

Another relevant archetype for women is the Goddess. Psychiatrist Jean Shinoda Bolen has written two excellent books on this subject, *Goddesses in Everywoman* and *Goddesses in Older Women*. In the first book, Bolen uses the goddesses and myths of ancient Greece to explore the Goddess archetypes that are active in younger women's lives. She believes that each of us is born with specific tendencies that vary according to which archetypes are active in us, and these patterns help shape our personalities.

In her second book, Bolen observes that in later postmenopausal years, women not only experience a biological change but also an internal shift in their psyches. Bolen writes about her entry into this stage in her life as a way to inspire women to become what she calls "green and juicy crones." For her, a green and juicy crone has a life that is soul-satisfying, a life that is predicated on making choices that lead internally to the authentic, true self.

Scholar, playwright, and storyteller Donna Wilshire, in her book *Virgin, Mother, Crone: Myths and Mysteries of the Triple Goddess*, describes three aspects of the ancient goddess, each of which is a reflection of the functions and roles of ordinary women. The Virgin or Maiden aspect of the goddess represents her cosmic life-giving aspect. The Mother, or Nurturer, is the aspect of the goddess that gives nourishment and sustenance for life. The Crone or Death-Bringer aspect of the goddess reclaims all forms of life, reshapes and transforms them into new possibilities, which she then gives birth to. Thus the triple form of the goddess is a mirror for the sacred cycle of birth/death/rebirth found throughout the cosmos.

As contemporary women age, especially those of us in the baby boom generation, it is important that we reconnect with these healthy, positive female archetypes. We need to challenge and shift the old negative stereotypes of elder women and understand the relationship between the denigration of women and the rape of Mother Earth. We need to remember our true potential as wise women, comfortable with our aging and sage-ing. Since we can no longer create new life, we can turn to our imaginations and with our hands rekindle the fires of creativity in a new way. By calling on our Wild Woman or Goddess archetypes to guide us, teach us, and empower us, we can find the courage to make the choices that will lead us back to our Selves as Whole, unmasked and real.

It is a journey that we can share with other women who are on the same path. Together we can continue to grow spiritually and psychologically, joining in women's circles to share our emotions and dreams, our struggles and experiences as women of the earth, and our deepest desires for wholeness. Coming together, we can explore the many things that we share and have in common as women—those things that we value as sacred and holy. As we gather in circles to bead, we can share our stories and find within them a common link. We can share our laughter and use humor as a means of lightening the load of our lives.

By learning to be fully present in each moment, we can release old "false selves" that no longer serve us. We can learn to make wise choices for ourselves. Each time we stir the pot, new doorways will open for us. We have only this moment, *Now!* How will we choose to live it?

Choices

When I am teaching beading classes, I often tell my students that beading is a metaphor for life. One example that often comes up has to do with choosing which beads to use: what colors, sizes, shapes, textures? When students ask me what I think they should use, I respond by asking, "What do *you* think and feel is right for this project, in this moment, now?" This often leads to a discussion about making choices. Personal choice can be scary. Some would prefer to have others make choices for them rather than make them for themselves, fearing they might make a mistake or create something they consider "less than perfect." Since I teach mostly women, I do not know if men feel so strongly about fearing choices or making what they perceive of as a mistake. This is certainly an issue for many women, however.

Life is made up of choices that are always available to us. They are not necessarily right or wrong choices, though they could be perceived as such. Another way of looking at a choice is to imagine it as coming to a crossroads. If we make *this* choice, it will lead us in one direction; if we make *that* choice, it will lead us in another direction. Rather than asking, "Which is the right choice?" the better question is, "What are the consequences of each choice, and which would I prefer in this present moment?"

The beading process is all about making choices. In my teaching, I work with students to help them rely on their own inner wisdom and gain the confidence to trust their own choices. I remind them—and myself—that beading brings us into the present moment where we can be open to what Eckart Tolle refers to in *The Power of Now* as the "clear space of infinite possibilities" and learn to make decisions joyfully. This is playing in the Creative Spirit! We can learn to release the limitations of thinking in terms of right/wrong duality and just have fun. Try this bead in this color, in this shape and texture, and see what happens. Ask the question, *What if … ?* and see where it leads you. Let go of expectations—

expectations of yourself, expectations of others. Learn to trust your own wisdom instead of looking outside of yourself for answers. Beading as a creative process can assist you in dealing with all of these issues.

Beading teaches me these lessons over and over again. I often sit with a piece in the morning and look at its colors and designs. Then I choose the colors to work with that day that feel right both for me and for the piece in that moment. I know that on another day, I might choose other colors because they would be what I needed to work with that day. This internal dialog continues in my beadwork. I rarely design a piece ahead of time. I allow each form to evolve from within myself, trusting that through this creative process, the piece will make itself through my hands. I become a hollow reed as I allow Spirit to flow through me while I create my beaded forms, and I trust that each piece will have its own perfection of color, form, and technique.

Choice has become a welcome visitor in my studio, and I hope you will welcome her to your beading work, as well. Before you start the projects in this chapter, I invite you to take time to do an exercise in focusing. I offer it as a way to help you be fully present to yourself so you can make wise choices. The purpose of focusing is to bring a conscious awareness to your body, to identify what is happening, to ask some questions and get some answers from your body. This can be especially helpful when you are having an emotional reaction to something, or when you need to make an important choice. Philosopher Eugene Gendlin first defined this process in his book *Focusing,* in which he describes focusing as a process of making contact with a special kind of internal bodily awareness that he calls a "felt sense." According to influential American author, editor, and public speaker Marilyn Ferguson, who wrote the Introduction to Gendlin's book, when we experience this felt sense shifting internally, it is essentially identical to the freeing insight of the creative process.

EXERCISE

Focusing—The Sacred Triangle

You can use this exercise to help you find answers within yourself about choices you are faced with, whether they are core internal issues or more mundane choices, such as what bead colors to work with on any given day. The central idea is "The Sacred Triangle," a concept introduced to me by one of my teachers, Jane Winyoté Ely. The exercise involves putting yourself in three different positions as you consider your choices.

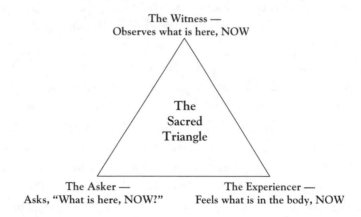

1. Find a place where you can sit in silence and not be disturbed.
2. Take some deep breaths, releasing tension on the exhalation. Relax your brow, jaw, and shoulders.
3. Come fully into this moment, now, and continue to watch your breath going in and out.
4. Set your intention to be in a sacred relationship with yourself. This is a "time out" for you, a time to be with yourself during which you can open yourself up to space, patience, and nonjudgment.

5. When you are ready, follow these six movements or steps involved in focusing:

1. Clear a space

Ask yourself these questions: "How is my life going? What is the main thing for me right now? What is between me and feeling fine?" (the position of the Asker). Do not answer; let what comes into your body do the answering (the position of the Witness). Sense within your body for the answers (the position of the Experiencer). Greet each concern that comes, putting it aside as you keep asking, "Except for that, am I fine?"

2. Felt sense

From among the things that came, select one issue to focus on. What do you sense in your body when you recall the whole of this issue? Let yourself sense all of this, the whole thing, the murky discomfort or the unclear body-sense of it. Begin to identify this issue and ask yourself, "Where is this feeling in my body?"

3. Get a handle

Identify the qualities of this unclear felt sense. What one word, phrase, or image comes out of this felt sense? Keep going until you have a match between the felt sense and its quality.

4. Resonate

Go back and forth between the felt sense and the word or phrase, checking on how they resonate with one another until you are sure they fit and capture the quality of the felt sense. Keep asking, "Is that right?" When you get a match between the words, image, or phrase with your felt sense, let yourself feel that for a minute. (You can keep moving around the positions of the Sacred Triangle while you are doing this.)

5. Ask

Silently ask, "What is it about the whole issue that makes me so _____?" (Insert the quality you have found into this sentence.) If you feel stuck, ask these questions:

- What is the worst of this feeling?
- What is really so bad about this?
- What does it need?
- What should happen?

Do not try to "manufacture" an answer; rather, wait for the feeling to stir and give you an answer.

6. Receive insight

Welcome whatever comes. Stay with this shift for a few moments. Know that it is only one step in understanding this issue and that you can continue with more focusing if you need additional clarity.

Before you begin to bead, I suggest you take a few minutes to use this meditation to bring you into a calm and focused state of being. In our frenetic daily life, we often do not take the time to bring ourselves into the present moment or to slow down and ask Spirit for guidance. This meditation will help you achieve this and guide you in setting the intention for your project.

Beginning Meditation

1. Sit comfortably with your feet on the floor and your spine straight.
2. Hold the stick or branch you have chosen for this project gently in one hand and close your eyes.
3. Take three deep breaths, releasing the tension inside your body with each exhalation.
4. Relax your jaw, your brow, your shoulders, and your stomach. Notice if there are other places in your body where you are tense; breathe into them consciously in order to release this tension.
5. Focus your attention on the Third Eye spiritual center between your eyebrows.

6. Imagine a clear white light emanating from this sacred center and radiating throughout your entire body. Bathe in this beautiful light as it envelops you in its healing powers.

7. You can direct this spiritual energy anywhere in your body. Bring it into your heart, and then send it throughout your body as you feel yourself expanding and becoming charged with its energy.

8. With your eyes still closed, bring your awareness to the stick you are holding in your hand. Can you feel its energy field?

9. Direct the clear white light from your Third Eye center through your heart, down through your arms and hands, and into the little wooden stick.

10. Silently state your intention to make a beaded goddess figure using this piece of wood as an armature.

11. Ask Spirit for guidance and direction in your project. In meditative silence, listen for any answers that might be given to you.

12. If you have any specific questions, ask them now and wait for the answers. As you wait, keep your focus on your breath, observing each inhalation and exhalation.

13. Ask Spirit for a special blessing on this project.

14. Ask Spirit to bless you, as the maker, and your hands that will be doing the beading.

15. Imagine pure love radiating out through your hands as you work on this project, infusing all that you touch with its healing powers.

16. When this feels complete, open your eyes and notice how you are feeling. If you have received any specific guidance during the meditation, you may want to write it down in your journal.

PROJECT 5
Goddess Archetype Necklace

MATERIALS

- Japanese seed beads, size 11, approximately 20 grams; size 8, approximately 10 grams
- Goddess pendant with bail or jump ring (You might have to search around to locate a goddess pendant. Over the years, I have found goddess pendants in carved turquoise, sodalite, ceramic, silver, pewter, various stones, and bone. If you search "goddess pendants" on the Internet, you will find a number of sites selling them. Also, Ebay is a good place to check for them. Make sure the pendant comes with either a jump ring or bail.)
- Button with shank
- Sharps short beading needles, size 12
- Silamide thread size A or Nymo thread size B
- Optional: cube beads, 4 millimeter, or gemstone chips
- Scissors
- Beading mat
- Ott light or desk lamp

Goddess Archetype Necklaces,
Wendy Ellsworth, 2008.
(For a color photograph of this project, see color plate 3b.)

PROJECT PREPARATION

- Pull off approximately 9 feet of thread and prestretch it by pulling it out between your hands, working your way along its entire length.
- Add a needle to your thread, bringing it close to the midpoint. You will want to work this stitch using a single width of the thread rather than double because of the number of times you will be passing back through the core beads.

Spiral Rope Chain Stitch

Spiral rope chain stitch has become a popular stitch to use in making beaded necklaces. It is easy to learn and works up quickly. It consists of beads that form the inner core of the stitch, often in a larger size, and beads that spiral around this central core, often a smaller size than the core beads. After the initial step that establishes the beginning of this necklace, each stitch consists of one core bead and multiple spiral beads. You can customize any necklace to make your own design by changing the size of the core beads as well as the size, shape, color, and number of spiral beads.

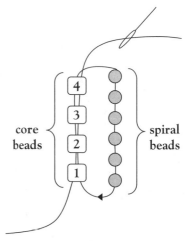

3.1. Spiral rope chain stitch, step 1.

STEP 1

(see figure 3.1)

- Pick up four size-8 seed beads (these are the "core beads") and six size-11 seed beads (these are the "spiral beads") and bring them down to the end of your thread, leaving a 12-inch tail to be used for the clasp.
- Pass the needle back through all four size-8 core beads a second time in the same direction, from bottom to top.

STEP 2

(see figure 3.2)

- Pick up one size-8 core bead (bead 5) and six size-11 spiral beads.
- Pass the needle back through the top three size-8 core beads, from bottom to top (beads 2–4), *and* the new core bead just added (bead 5).
- You have now completed one spiral rope chain stitch.

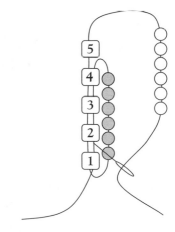

3.2. Spiral rope chain stitch, step 2.

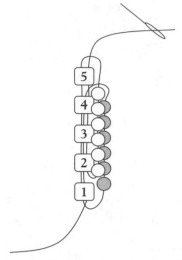

3.3. Spiral rope chain stitch, step 3.

STEP 3

(see figure 3.3)

- Push the spiral beads around to the back of the core beads counterclockwise. You will need to do this for every stitch so they are in the correct position before starting the next stitch.

STEP 4

- Continue to add beads in the same sequence as step 2, passing back through the last three core beads in the base row and the core bead just added in the stitch you are finishing.
- Be sure to push the spiral beads around to the back of the core beads in the same direction (counterclockwise) after completing every stitch (step 3). If you are left-handed, it will probably be easier for you to push the spiral beads to the back of the core beads clockwise.

VARIATIONS

- You may choose to use 4-millimeter cube beads in the middle of every third row of the spiral beads as a different design element. You may also choose to use gemstone chips in the center of the necklace as the spiral beads for added interest.
- If you want to include a 4-millimeter cube bead as a variation, here is a possible sequence: Pick up one size-8 core bead, two size-11 seed beads, one 4-millimeter cube bead, and two size-11 seed beads and work the stitch as described in step 3.
- To substitute gemstone chips for the size-11 spiral beads, here is a possible sequence: Pick up one size-8 core bead and three or four gemstone chips, and work the stitch as described in step 3. You want the measurement of the gemstone chips to equal the measurement of six size-11 seed beads, so you may have to alter the number of gemstone clips from my suggested amount of three or four. (Each of the necklaces in color plate 3b show gemstone chips in the center of the necklace.)

Changing Thread

(see figure 3.4)

You will have to add a new thread when you get close to the end of the thread you are working with. There are many ways to add a new thread, but the one I often use is to tie the new thread to the old one before ending the old thread. To do this:

- Complete a stitch (steps 2 and 3) so that your old thread is coming out of the top core bead. Set the necklace aside for the moment.
- Pull off a new length of thread and add a needle to it, following the directions for Project Preparation.
- Weave this new thread through at least five of the core beads below where you stopped working (on figure 3.4, these are beads 1–5).
- After stitching through three of the five core beads, tie a simple overhand slip knot around the threads passing through these beads.
- Leave a small tail sticking out of the first core bead you stitch into, which you will cut off once the thread is secure.
- Both the new thread and the old thread should now be coming out of the top of the top core bead (bead 1 in figure 3.4), side by side. Tie the new thread to the old thread using a square knot.
- Take the old thread and stitch down through the spiral beads of the final stitch. Cut it off to end it.
- Cut off the tail of the new thread.
- Continue beading with the new thread.

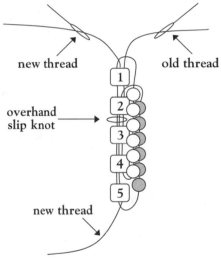

3.4. Changing thread.

GODDESS PENDANT

- When the necklace is half the length you want it to be, add the goddess pendant by passing one stitch of the spiral beads through the jump ring or bail attached to the pendant before stitching into the core beads. This will allow your pendant to hang in the middle of your necklace. (See color plate 3b.)
- Continue beading the second half of the necklace until the other side is the same length as the first side.

Clasp
(see figure 3.5)

- At one end of the necklace, add a button with shank. To do this, pick up three seed beads, pass through the shank of the button, and pick up three more beads.
- Stitch back down into the top core bead, exiting from the fifth bead from the top.
- Pass back through the spiral beads and the top core bead and through all the loop beads and button shank a second time. You can repeat this one more time if you can get your needle though all the beads.
- End your thread by tying several overhand knots around the core thread and weaving the end into a few more beads.

FINISHING

- At the opposite end of the necklace, pick up enough beads to make a loop that fits over the button you have chosen.
- To do this, stitch back down into the top core bead, exiting from the fifth bead from the top.
- Pass back through the spiral beads and the top core bead and through all the loop beads a second time. (See figure 3.5.)

3.5. Adding button with shank for clasp.

- You can repeat this one more time if you can get your needle though all the beads.
- End your thread by tying several overhand knots around the core thread and weaving the end into a few more beads.

◉ ◉ ◉

PROJECT 6
Beaded Stick Figure Goddess

These directions are for beading in tubular gourd (peyote) stitch. For my beaded stick figures, I use this stitch almost exclusively. It is very versatile, easy to increase and decrease, and covers the wood like a second skin. However, you can use any beading technique(s) that you are comfortable with to bead around the stick.

Beaded Stick Figure Goddess,
Wendy Ellsworth, 1994. (For a color photograph of this project, see color plate 4a.)

MATERIALS

- Small tree stick or branch that resembles a human torso
- Seed beads, size 11, in colors of your choice
- Embellishment beads or other materials you want to use, such as shells, leather, buttons, bells, feathers, gemstones, crystals
- Sharps short beading needles, size 12
- Silamide thread size A or Nymo thread size B, in colors to match beads
- Scissors
- Beading mat
- Sharp pocket knife
- Ott light or desk lamp
- Journal
- Pen or pencil

PROJECT PREPARATION

- Use the knife to skin the bark off the tree branch and shape it, if desired.
- Pull off approximately 4 feet of thread and prestretch. If possible, work the thread doubled. If not, work it single width.
- Add needle to thread; bring to the middle of the thread if working doubled.

TUBULAR GOURD STITCH

- It takes four rows to establish the stitch.

Base Row

(this base will form rows 1 and 2)

- Decide where you want to start the beading. You can begin at the top of the stick or in the middle.
- Pick up enough beads to wrap entirely around the stick wherever you begin beading. Try to use an odd number of beads rather than even.
- Tie the thread with the beads on it into a square knot around the stick. If you leave a long tail, you can add a needle onto it later to start beading in the opposite direction or to end off. (You can wrap the tail around a small piece of cardboard to secure it and keep it out of the way.)
- Stitch back through the first bead that you picked up on the thread originally (going in the same direction). Being right-handed, I stitch from right to left, in a clockwise manner.

Row 3

(see figure 3.6)

- Begin row 3 by picking up a single bead, skipping over the next bead in sequence on the base row, and passing the needle through the next bead (bead 3).
- Continue to pick up a bead, skip a bead, and pass through the next bead all the way around the base row until you get back to the first bead of row 3.

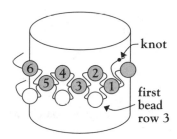

3.6. Tubular gourd stitch, row 3.

Row 4

(see figure 3.7)

- Begin row 4 by picking up a bead and stitching into the second bead of row 3. The bead will fit into the gap between beads 1 and 2 of row 3. (They are not numbered in the diagram.)

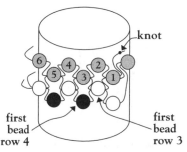

3.7. Tubular gourd stitch, row 4.

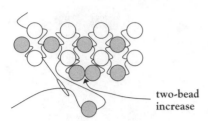

3.8. Increasing in gourd stitch, step 1.

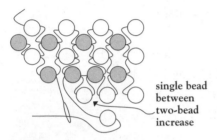

3.9. Radical increase in gourd stitch, step 2.

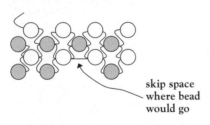

3.10. Decreasing in gourd stitch, step 1.

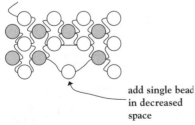

3.11. Decreasing in gourd stitch, step 2.

- Continue to put a single bead in each gap as you work your way around the row. Each row will lead directly into the next one, and the first bead of each row will move one position to the left.

Increasing and Decreasing

- Continue to bead the stick in tubular gourd stitch until you have covered as much of the surface of the stick as you want. Because the surface of the wood is irregular, you will need to increase and decrease as needed. Both increasing and decreasing take two steps each.

Increasing: Step 1

(see figure 3.8)

- Pick up two beads instead of a single bead and take a stitch into the next bead.

Increasing: Step 2

(see figure 3.9)

- When you come back to this two-bead increase in the subsequent row, stitch into the first bead of the two-bead increase, pick up a single bead, and stitch into the second bead of the increase. This is referred to as a "radical" increase.

Decreasing: Step 1

(see figure 3.10)

- To decrease, skip a space where a bead would normally be placed.

Decreasing: Step 2

(see figure 3.11)

- In the subsequent row, place a single bead in the decreased space and tighten the tension on the thread to make it tight.

BEADING A "CROTCH"

When you come to a "crotch" in the wood, you will need to improvise. Try starting a new row of beads on each "leg"; then join the beads from the legs to the beads from the "trunk" of the figure. It will take several rows to make the two parts meet one another. Experiment! It is really not that hard when you are in the process of figuring it out on the piece.

Crotch detail, *Stick Figure Goddess*, Wendy Ellsworth, 1994.

INTERACTIVE PROCESS

As you work on the piece, create a dialog with it. Notice your thoughts and feelings; you may want to keep track of them in your journal. Let this be an interactive process of self-discovery as you are beading and working. Try to keep a neutral position regarding your thoughts and feelings, overriding the urge to label them as good or bad, positive or negative. Let yourself just *be*, fully present in each moment as you pick up each bead.

EMBELLISHMENT

After you have covered the surface of the wood in gourd stitch, you may want to embellish your stick figure goddess by adding other materials. Maybe you want to add on a skirt, a headdress, or a necklace? What does the piece need for completion? For my stick figure *Stands Tall Woman,* I added a leather skirt embellished with beads and dentalium shells, a piece of shell in both of her "hands," and feathers from a ruffed grouse as a headdress.

Stands Tall Woman, Wendy Ellsworth, 36 x 30 x 6½ inches, glass seed beads, dentalium shells, sea shells, leather, feathers, wooden stick, redwood base, 1994. (Photograph by George Erml.)

◉ ⊙ ◎

Ending Meditation

1. Find a space and a time when you can sit quietly with your completed project. Have your journal beside you.
2. You may want to light a candle and smudge yourself and your stick figure goddess.
3. If possible, hold your completed project in your hands or place her in front of you.
4. Sit with a straight spine and your feet flat on the floor.
5. Close your eyes and take at least three deep breaths, releasing all the tension of the day, allowing yourself to become present with your breath.
6. Bring your attention to the Third Eye center between your brows. Imagine a beautiful, clear white light emanating from here.
7. Bring this white light down into your heart and send it into the rest of your body with love.
8. Surround your goddess stick figure with this radiant light and empower it with your love.
9. Are there any messages this goddess figure has to share with you? Ask her and wait for an answer (Spirit moves in wondrous ways). Dialog with her until the process feels complete.
10. Thank her and the Wild Woman archetype within yourself that assisted you in making this goddess figure. Thank yourself for having the courage to say "Yes!" to the challenge of using beading as a life art process.
11. Thank Spirit for the guidance you received while completing this project.
12. When ready, open your eyes and observe the creativity you are holding in your hands.

13. Use your journal to record your emotions and thoughts and anything else that came to you in this concluding meditation.

Spin the Wheels of Life

For Integration and Wholeness

The chakras are our spiritual archive.
—Caroline Shinola Arewa

The Chakra System

Ever since I began beading, my work has been directly connected to my inner search for spiritual meaning. I have used my bead art to explore many aspects of my sacred journey. One area of primary interest that I have explored through beadwork is the chakra system of the body.

The philosophy of the chakra system dates back to oral traditions that precede the ancient texts of India known as the Vedas. The word *chakra* comes from the Sanskrit language and translates as "wheel" or "disk"; it is a way of explaining how the human system works. Traditional Hindu teachings describe a chakra as a wheel of energy that spins within different levels of the human energy field and is instrumental in metabolizing energy from what is considered the universal energy field. According to the theory of the chakra system, each person has seven major chakras that together make up a system for wholeness that integrates

93

Seven major chakras.

body, mind, and spirit. Spiritual coach and author Caroline Shola Arewa writes in her book *Opening to Spirit* that the chakras form the energetic core of the human organism, and she refers to the chakras as our "gift of divinity."

The chakra energy centers can help us understand how ideas, starting from the realm of Spirit, become concrete physical objects such as our beautiful beaded creations. Think of the chakras as conductors of energy, drawing down cosmic energy into the body in a downward flow that moves from the unmanifested into the physical realm. Or the energy can flow in reverse, drawing up from the earth, circulating energy through the body, and transmuting it into spiritual awareness.

Each of the chakras play a vital role in bringing our constructive ideas into existence and is an integral part of every concept that we wish to develop. If any of our chakras are blocked, it might not be possible to follow the creative process through to completion, or at the very least we might run into difficulties that slow down the progression from start to finish.

Each chakra has a specific meaning, location in the body, function, Sanskrit name, associated element, inner states of being, color, and sound. Our chakras can be open, closed, distorted, or still—conditions that affect our wellness either positively or negatively. The chakra system can play a vital role in understanding our overall physical health, as well as our emotional and mental well-being. By learning where we are blocking the flow of energy through our chakras and releasing those blocks, we can come back into balance, wholeness, and health.

I have found multiple ways to incorporate the wisdom of the chakra system into my bead art, in chakra necklaces, chakra brooches, chakra earrings, and chakra bracelets. I once designed a chakra sculpture in seven layers and beaded each layer in the primary color associated with that specific chakra, with a gemstone set into the center held in place by a beaded bezel. (See Project 8 at the end of this chapter.) I made two sets of these three-dimensional sculptures and photographed them together as if they were two people in relationship with each other, showing both attraction to and rejection of one another. I also teach classes in which participants make a beaded necklace while learning about the chakra system. Following the sequence of the colors of the rainbow, each Chakra Necklace becomes a reflection of the chakra system of its maker. (See Project 7 at the end of this chapter.)

Beading the Seven Chakras

Since the projects for this chapter are based on the chakra system, I want to give you some information about the main characteristics of each chakra. Though most sources describe the chakras from the Root chakra up through the Crown chakra, I have chosen to present the chakras in *descending* order because I feel it is important to our creative beadwork to track more deeply how we use the Creative Spirit to bring an idea through the chakra system. There is a downward flow of core energy that begins with inspiration (*in Spiritus*) and ends with the physical reality, the creative work of our hands. I hope this information helps you become more aware of how the theory of this subtle energy system works. It is a model that I work with daily as I consciously bring my bead art to life through this descending, creative process.

Chakra 7: The Crown Chakra

To get a good sense of the seventh chakra, imagine a cone-shaped spinning vortex that begins at the top of your head and extends upward approximately two to three feet in height. This is the Crown chakra, with its almost indescribably beautiful shimmering colors that change from violet to white and into gold. The frequencies of these colors are very high and are represented in the Sanskrit chakra system as the thousand-petal lotus flower, or

Chakra seven.

Sahasrara. This is the seat of what Canadian psychologist Richard Bucke termed "cosmic consciousness."

The main function of the Crown chakra is a connection to our Source, the Divine Spirit, or God. It is a state of physical, mental, emotional, and spiritual integration. We can also connect with the inner states of the Crown chakra: blissfulness, spiritual love, peace, harmony, and joy. This is the level at which we can understand the "bigger picture" of our life experiences that gives us a sense of unity and wholeness, a knowing that we are connected to all that is.

Our creative ideas have their genesis in our Crown chakra. They begin with a yearning to create a new form, a desire to give birth to a new idea. This yearning opens us up to the potential of what is possible. Think of this yearning as a vibration that goes out through the Crown chakra like a ripple into the cosmos. Universal intelligence responds to this vibration, and the descending current of energy begins to flow through us. In her book *Wheels of Life: A User's Guide to the Chakra System,* leading authority on the chakra system Anodea Judith refers to this birth of ideas before they take physical form as "conception." According to Judith, "conception" gives us the pattern, while "manifestation" fills it with substance and gives it form.

During the period when I was making beaded leather handbags, I was often commissioned to make a purse for a client. I truly enjoyed making these custom-designed purses because the beaded imagery was usually left up to my inspiration. If I knew the person, I would hold a mental image of her in my mind as I sat quietly and meditated on her purse. I would clear my mind of all other thoughts and then send out a question to the universe, asking for guidance and direction for a beaded design that would be appropriate for my client. As I waited for an image to "download" into my mind's eye, I could feel the excitement building inside of me. Inspiration can be rapturous at times! When the image I was waiting for emerged, I would be filled with the joy that comes with the initial conception of a new idea. This is how we can use the Crown chakra, in conjunction with the Creative Spirit, to bring a new idea into consciousness so it can begin its journey into physical manifestation.

Chakra 6: Third Eye Center

As with each of the chakras, the sixth chakra is a cone-shaped vortex through which we receive and transmit energy to and from the universal energy field. Its color is a deep indigo blue, and it is called the Third Eye center because of its location slightly above and between the eyebrows. This is the center through which we create our reality and through which the universe can mirror back to

Chakra six.

us our beliefs, either positive or negative. It is the center that powers our thoughts, our memories, and our attitudes. This is where we either limit ourselves from a place of narrow-mindedness or allow ourselves to expand and grow in higher awareness and deeper understanding.

The seat of wisdom is located in the sixth chakra. This is the center through which we can discern the kernels of truth that lie within every experience we have ever had, learn to forgive ourselves for our mistakes, and take responsibility for our lives. When we examine ourselves and our life's experiences so as to gain a deeper understanding from them, we are on the path to acquiring wisdom.

It is also in the sixth chakra that the seed of the idea we have conceived of in the Crown chakra begins to take form and shape. This is when we get to play around with the idea in our mind to see if it is actually something we can work with. Medical intuitive Caroline Myss writes in her book *Sacred Contracts: Awakening Your Divine Potential* that we use the sixth chakra to evaluate our idea intellectually in order to decide whether we want to manage the birth of our idea into its physical form.

Whenever I would receive an inspiration during meditation for a beaded design for a commissioned purse, I would begin to examine it in as much detail as possible in my mind's eye—the sixth chakra. I would toss it around in my thoughts to see if it was a "fit" with my client. If it became clear that it was a match with my client and would be something that I would enjoy creating for her, I would end my meditation, thanking Spirit for giving me guidance.

Chakra 5: Throat Chakra

Chakra five.

The location of the fifth chakra is at our throat, and its color is a radiant cerulean or turquoise blue. One of its main functions is communication. Anodea Judith calls communication the "coordinating principle of all life." It makes life possible, from the cellular level to the words that finally come out of our open mouths. Communication connotes sound, and sound is vibration. There is an ancient Hindu belief that the universe was manifested from a single sound vibration: *AUM*. This philosophy has an interesting parallel in the Christian belief that "in the beginning was the Word."

The fifth chakra is also one of the seats of creative expression in our body. This is key for us as beaders because our art is a form of creative expression, a way of communicating our ideas to others. It is in the fifth chakra that we translate symbolic imagery into concrete information that we can apply to our creative art forms.

When I was designing a purse for a client, once I had an idea for a beaded symbol or image, I would begin an inner dialog with myself, asking questions such as: What's the meaning of this symbol or image? How does it relate to my client? Is it appropriate for her purse? Do I think it works for this commission? What color choices would work for it? Do I want to include additional symbols or images? If so, what would they be? How can I combine them so that the design will be fully integrated?

I would usually sketch out the ideas that came to me so I would have a concrete image for reference. I would continue to mentally work out the concepts until I thought I had enough clarity to be able to express these ideas to my client, both verbally and visually.

Chakra 4: Heart Chakra

The fourth chakra is referred to as the Heart chakra because it is located in the area of the heart in our physical body. Its colors are scintillating green and rose pink. It is the central chakra, and it mediates between the energy centers below it and above it. Its task is to integrate and balance the energy flowing throughout our entire body; it is a bridge through which the energy flows in both directions.

Chakra four.

The human heart is where we hold tenderness, kindness, and empathy. It is here that we open to the lessons of love and compassion, for ourselves and for others. There are many different types of love: *agape*, which means to love your neighbor as yourself; *eros*, which is a purely physical, sexual attraction between two people; *amor,* which is love that comes from two people looking into one another's eyes and feeling the lightning bolt of mutual attraction from head to toe.

There is another description of love that is quite different from these three: "Love is living each moment to its highest potential." As the teacher who gave me this definition, Nancy Doyne, went on to explain, "Oftentimes, this form of love won't feel much like love." Perhaps this definition comes closest to helping us get a grasp on how love relates to the creative process. If we are able to live each moment to its highest potential, we will be fully present in each moment. And when we are fully present and pushing the envelope of creative energy, completely absorbed with the act of creation, we tap into a well of infinite potential that is ecstatic and euphoric. Love is the fuel that ignites and sustains this creative process.

It is at the Heart chakra level that we develop a relationship and bond with our beaded project. We embrace it, become passionate about it, get excited about it, and know that it is something we want to create. We get completely "turned on."

Often, as I was working on a beaded purse design, I would bring the symbol or image I had chosen into my Heart chakra in order to develop a loving, caring relationship with it. I would embrace and surround it with positive energy, allowing it to grow as if it were a beautiful plant just starting to bud. I would be full of anticipation and excitement about its progress. I knew that the blossoming stage was yet to come, and by energizing it with my love and passion, it would continue to grow and flourish. I was using the loving energies from my Heart chakra to develop a bond with my new idea, which would provide the impetus to see it through to completion. It is said that through love all things are possible!

Chakra 3: Solar Plexus

The third chakra, located in our solar plexus, relates to our sense of self: self-worth, self-esteem, and self-confidence. Its color is a vibrant, deep yellow, and it is our "fire in the belly." It relates to our personal power, our ego, and personal identity. Its purpose is transformation through the power of our will—our willpower. It also controls the metabolism of energy in our bodies and relates directly to how we digest food—and new ideas. It corresponds to our gut instincts and our true feelings.

Chakra three.

Many of us are cut off from our real feelings and have learned to rely on our intellectual acuity instead. Many people *think* their feelings rather than *feel* them. A friend of mine used to describe herself as "a head on a plate," in acknowledgment of how disconnected she was from her emotions. This pattern gets set up early in life if we do not get support to express our feelings, and we can begin to shut down emotionally. This often leads to disempowerment and feelings of self-doubt, guilt, and shame.

I encourage my students to use beading as a means of developing a positive self-esteem. Beading can and does provide a method for accessing our deepest feelings of personal self-worth and self-confidence as we play in the creative process. It can regenerate our inner fire in the belly—our passion. Completing a beautiful piece of beadwork can help us regain confidence in our ability to be creative and help restore our sense of personal power.

In my beaded purse work, once I embraced the beaded design I had selected, I would bring it to the level of my Solar Plexus chakra in order to empower it. This is what I call walking to the edge of a cliff and jumping off. Each beaded creation I have made has in many ways represented a giant leap of faith on my part into the unknown world of the Creative Spirit. Because each piece I make is unique, every time I work through the creative process using the seven chakras, I find that I need to go through this step in order to overcome any doubt I might have about not being able to complete my project.

I might spend some time with my design, observing how I feel about it and asking myself: Am I feeling challenged? Am I feeling excited? Am I feeling a bit fearful? Do I feel good about the design? Do I feel frustrated that it is taking too long just to get it to the place where I can get started on it? How do I feel about the colors I have chosen for the piece? What is the tone I am looking to create in my design? Is my design balanced?

This process not only connects me with my gut feelings, but also gives me the courage to trust my creative energy. After considering my response to these questions, I would be "fired up" with the will to proceed with my project. This is how we can use the Solar Plexus chakra to come to terms with how we feel about our creative ideas and where we develop the willpower to push our ideas through to manifestation.

Chakra 2: Sacral Chakra

The second chakra is also known as the Sacral chakra. Its color is an iridescent orange. Its location in the body encompasses the entire pelvic region and includes our sexual organs. This is where our levels of sensuality, sexuality, and reproduction are held. It is the home of pleasure, which is essential for the health of our bodies. It is also the center for our emotions. I think of "e-motion" as energy into motion. This connotes movement, and it is through movement that we bring about change. Movement and change are the two basic elements of the second chakra.

Our center of gravity, or Tan T'ien, resides in the second chakra and is our point of balance, internal and external. When we connect with this place of balance, it will be reflected into our outer lives. We will feel calmer, more centered and peaceful, and better able to handle what we have set into motion.

Chakra two.

The second chakra is another center of personal creativity. This is where our creative juices really begin to flow through our beaded project, energizing it with a charge of "e-motion." Creativity, like sexuality, is an important, vital aspect of our essential nature; the desire to procreate exists within each of us, female and male. Birthing a new art form can be as physically, emotionally, mentally, and spiritually exhausting as birthing a baby. While our ideas are in the womb of the second chakra, they go through a similar gestation period before being brought through the birth canal into the light. We get to decide how long the gestation period will last as our idea incubates in our watery womb of potentiality. Then we will begin the birthing process, the long journey down the dark canal toward the light of the physical world. The reward of this sometimes painful process can be feelings of ecstatic euphoria and joy.

Whenever I was making a purse for a client, during this gestation phase I would often "clean house" or "feather my nest," both activities common to women about to give birth to a new baby. For me, this would involve preparing my studio space before I began the physical work on the piece. I would start by removing any unnecessary clutter so I would have a clean, clear surface on which to work. I would pull beads that I needed for the project off of my shelves and place them in little piles on my leather beading mat. I would place needles, thread, wax, scissors, and pliers to the side, where I had easy access to them. I would turn on the heat or air conditioning for comfort, choose CDs according to my mood, fill my water fountain, and light incense. Finally, I would do a chakra exercise, visualizing the vertical currents of core energy as they flowed through my body, grounding the descending current through the Root chakra deep into Mother Earth and sending the ascending current out my Crown chakra into the spiritual realms. Thus balanced, I was ready for the labor of love to begin. I was ready to give birth to my new idea. My beaded design was about to take form at last!

Chakra 1: Root Chakra

The first chakra is also known as the Root chakra. Its Sanskrit name, Muladhara, means "root support." This is the foundation of support for our physical bodies, located at the perineum, midway between the anus and genitals. Its element is Earth, from which we receive the nourishment that keeps our bodies healthy, active, and alive. The issues we deal with in this Root chakra have to do with our physical survival and self-preservation, as well as how we relate to our family, community, and tribe. Its color, a deep red, has the longest wavelength and slowest vibration in the visible color spectrum.

Chakra one.

When we are feeling out of alignment—stressed out, scattered, or unfocused—one way to regain our equilibrium is to ground our energy into the earth through our Root chakra. When we do this, we reconnect with the flow of vital energy that moves downward through us into the earth as well as upward through us into Spirit.

When we are grounded, we can "stand on our own two feet" and "stand up for ourselves." Mother Earth can give us a solid boundary to push against in order to define ourselves as individuated human beings. When we feel connected to the earth through our Root chakra, we can feel balanced, safe, and secure. It can give us energy that will vitalize others we come in contact with. It can also imbue us with a strong will to live and a strong "presence" of personal power.

When we bring our creative ideas to the level of our Root chakra, we give birth to them. We are ready to manifest and ground them into physicality. This is the time when we pick up our tools and finally get to work. If we are a wood turner, we attach a block of wood to the lathe, turn on the machine, and put the tool to the wood. If we are a potter, we take a hunk of clay, center it on our wheel, and pull the clay up into shape. If we are a glassblower, we turn on our furnaces, and when the glass is molten hot, we pick up a gather of glass on the end of our punty stick and begin to blow. If we are a bead artist, we thread our needle and begin to work with our beads, weaving them together to create the object we have so carefully designed.

When I would sit down to begin beading a design for a client, I would often close my eyes for a few moments before beginning and do a grounding exercise to bring myself into alignment with the purpose of creating my new project and to bring myself fully into the present moment. Then I would open my eyes and look over the beads I had chosen for my design. They often were in little piles placed around my beading mat, most likely in no particular order. Threading my needle, I would pick up the piece of leather on which I was going to bead and begin to work. If I was making a circular mandala, I would have already prestretched a piece of leather on an embroidery hoop. If I wanted to bead directly onto the surface of a purse, I would have already cut out all the pieces of the purse and drawn the outline of my design onto the front. Working quietly, I would allow myself to become completely absorbed in the creative energy of beading.

Beading is extremely labor intensive, and it takes many hours for a project to be completed. Because of this, I always invite Patience to become my muse. Thread that constantly twists and tangles, needles that bend and break, beads that crack when you pass through them a second or third time, shoulders that become tight, and low-back pain are all parts of this creative endeavor that require patience and perseverance. My beadwork takes days, weeks, sometimes months to complete! This is all Root chakra manifestation at work. No matter how long it takes to complete my finished object, I keep going because I know that the reward at the end will more than justify all the time it takes to bring my creation to completion.

◎◎◎

This is the journey through the chakras, bringing the concept of a beading project downward from the Crown chakra to the Root chakra, where we ground it into physicality. Now I am going to turn the process over to you. Each of the projects for this chapter will take you through the seven chakras on a journey of self-exploration. The first project is a lovely Chakra Necklace in the colors of the rainbow chakras. The second project is a beaded Chakra Flower Sculpture that contains seven layers, and each layer is the color of a chakra.

Before you begin each project, I have offered an exercise or meditation that will help you focus on your chakra energies. For the first project, the exercise is a visualization that is especially helpful if you are feeling stressed. It will help you discharge any negative energies you have and reconnect you with the positive core energies flowing through your body. Note how you feel before and after you do this visualization.

EXERCISE
Visualizing the Vertical Currents of Core Energy

STEP 1: ASCENDING CURRENT OF CORE ENERGY

1. Find a time when you will be undisturbed and quiet.
   You may want to smudge yourself before you begin. (See the exercise "Blessing the Materials" on p. 47.)

2. You can do this exercise either standing or seated comfortably in a chair. It is important that your spine be as straight as possible. Imagine that something is pulling the top of your head upward to make you stand or sit as tall as you can. If seated, make sure your feet are on the floor, legs uncrossed.

3. Consciously relax your face, your shoulders, and your abdomen, and begin to breathe deeply from your diaphragm. You may do this exercise with your eyes open or closed.

4. Begin to visualize energy from the earth gently flowing upward through your body, starting with your feet. Bring this energy from deep within the earth up through your feet, ankles, calves and thighs, into the base of your spine and genital area. Continue bringing the energy up through your abdomen, your solar plexus, and into your heart region. Breathe deeply as you feel this energy swirling around your heart and chest. Continue to bring the energy flow up through your throat, neck, and face, all the way to the top of your head; then send it out above your body into the universe.

5. Repeat this visualization as many times as you want until you truly connect with this flow of core energy running through your body from the earth upward and out the top of your head. Imagine it as a stream of water, washing you clean as it moves through you, releasing blocks and tension as it flows upward into the cosmos above you. Send the stream of energy all the way out to the stars and galaxies beyond as a gift to them from Mother Earth.

STEP 2: DESCENDING CURRENT OF CORE ENERGY

1. Now visualize a starting point somewhere above you, as far out into the stars or galaxies as you sent your ascending core energy. Imagine a current of energy originating from this distant point, and bring this energy down through the top of your head, through your face, your neck, and your throat, and into your heart area. Breathe deeply as this current continues to flow down through your heart, into your solar

plexus, abdomen, and genitals, down through your legs, knees, calves, ankles, and feet, and send it into the earth as deeply as you can imagine it going.

2. Repeat this visualization until you truly feel this current running through your body from above your head and down into the earth. Use your breath to help this flow of core energy unblock any places that feel stuck and give it to Mother Earth as good composting material. Imagine that you are grounding the light from the stars into Mother Earth, through your body.

Chakra Necklace

This is a simple necklace that uses the rainbow colors of the chakra system in a spiral rope chain stitch. As you pick up each color, remember that it corresponds directly to your own chakra system and has potentially beneficial healing effects for you.

MATERIALS

- Japanese seed beads, size 8, gold, 10 grams
- Czech True Cut seed beads, size 10, in eight colors: red, orange, yellow, dark green, turquoise blue, indigo blue, and violet, 5 grams each color (See the Resources section for where to purchase True Cut beads.)
- Silamide thread size A or Nymo thread size B, in neutral color
- Sharps short beading needles, size 12
- Clasp of choice (directions below show how to add a button with shank)
- Scissors
- Beading mat
- Ott light or desk lamp

Chakra Necklaces, Wendy Ellsworth, 2007.
(For a color photograph of this project, see color plate 4b.)

SPIRAL ROPE CHAIN STITCH

The process for making the spiral rope chain stitch follows the same steps that I described for the Goddess Archetype Necklace in chapter 3. The only difference is in the type of beads used for the spiral beads. For this project I am suggesting you use Czech True Cut seed beads in size 10. True Cut have a single facet cut into one side of the bead that makes them sparkle. Because they are Czech seed beads, they are smaller than a Japanese size 11, and thus the directions tell you to use a total of eight of them for the spiral beads, instead of the six you used for the Goddess Archetype Necklace.

PROJECT PREPARATION

- Pull off approximately 9 feet of thread and prestretch it by pulling it out between your hands, working your way along its entire length.
- Add a needle to your thread, bringing it close to the midpoint. You will want to work this stitch using a single width of the thread rather than double because of the number of times you will be passing back through the core beads.

STEP 1

(see figure 4.1)

- Pick up four size-8 seed beads (these are the "core beads") and eight size-10 True Cut beads (these are the "spiral beads"), and bring them down to the end of your thread, leaving a 12-inch tail to be used for the clasp. (If you would like to try different color sequences, see the variations on p. 110.)
- Pass the needle back through all four size-8 core beads a second time in the same direction, from bottom to top.

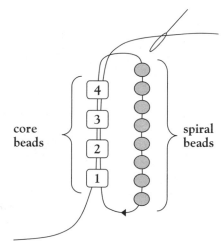

4.1. Spiral rope chain stitch, step 1.

STEP 2

(see figure 4.2)

- Pick up one size-8 core bead (bead 5) and eight size-10 True Cut spiral beads.
- Pass the needle back through the top three size-8 core beads, from bottom to top (beads 2–4), *and* the new core bead just added (bead 5).
- You have now completed one spiral rope chain stitch.

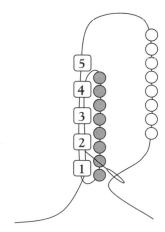

4.2. Spiral rope chain stitch, step 2.

Color Variations

You may choose to add the chakra colors in a variety of sequences. Here are three variations that I have found pleasing:

- Color sequence 1 (as shown in the top necklace in color plate 4b): pick up one size-8 seed bead for the core bead and eight True Cut beads for the spiral beads in the following sequence: two red, one orange, one yellow, one green, one turquoise blue, one indigo blue, one violet.
- Color sequence 2 (as shown in the bottom necklace in color plate 4b): pick up one size-8 seed bead for the core bead and eight True Cut beads for the spiral beads. Use a solid color of True Cut beads for each stitch, following the chakra system colors from the Root chakra up through the Crown chakra:

  Stitch 1: eight red beads (for chakra 1, the Root chakra)

  Stitch 2: eight orange beads (for chakra 2, the Sacral chakra)

  Stitch 3: eight yellow beads (for chakra 3, the Solar Plexus chakra)

  Stitch 4: eight green beads (for chakra 4, the Heart chakra)

  Stitch 5: eight turquoise or cerulean blue beads (for chakra 5, the Throat chakra)

  Stitch 6: eight indigo blue beads (for chakra 6, the Third Eye chakra)

  Stitch 7: eight violet beads (for chakra 7, the Crown chakra)

- Once you have completed seven stitches, repeat the sequence again and continue this for the entire necklace. For my necklace, which measured 26 inches, I repeated this sequence a total of thirty-five times.
- Color sequence 3 (as shown in the middle necklace in color plate 4b): In this sequence, the necklace will be made using whole segments of each color, following the chakra color sequence, starting with violet (that will be at both ends of the

necklace) and progressing to red (that will be in the middle of the necklace). You will need to decide how many stitches will comprise each color segment, as this will determine the overall length of the necklace. In the sample pictured for this project, I used fifteen stitches for each color segment (each with one core seed bead and eight True Cut spiral beads), starting with violet beads (for the Crown chakra) until I reached the red beads (for the Root chakra), which is at the center of the necklace. For the red beads, I doubled the count for a total of thirty stitches, keeping the total number of beads always the same (one core seed bead and eight True Cut spiral beads). Then I started back up the chakra colors, repeating the color segments of the first side of the necklace in reverse, ending with violet. My necklace measured a total of 24 inches.

STEP 3

(see figure 4.3)

- Push the spiral beads around to the back of the core beads counterclockwise.
- You will need to do this for every stitch so that they are in the correct position before starting the next stitch.

STEP 4

- Continue to add beads in the same sequence as step 2, passing back through the last three core beads in the base row and the core bead just added in the stitch you are finishing.
- Be sure to push the spiral beads around to the back of the core beads in the same direction (counterclockwise) after completing every stitch. (If you are left-handed, it will probably be easier for you to push the spiral beads to the back of the core beads clockwise.)

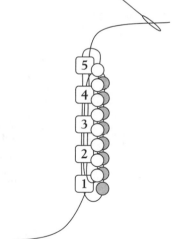

4.3. Spiral rope chain stitch, step 3.

Changing Thread
(see figure 4.4)

You will have to add a new thread when you get close to the end of the thread you are working with. There are many ways to add a new thread, but the one I always use is to tie the new thread to the old one before ending the old thread. To do this:

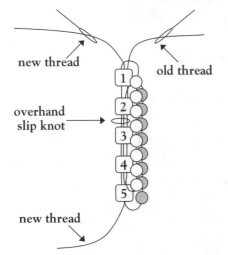

new thread

old thread

overhand
slip knot

new thread

4.4. Changing thread.

- Complete a stitch (step 2) so that your old thread is coming out of the top core bead.
- Set the necklace aside for the moment.
- Pull off a new length of thread and add a needle to it, following the directions for Project Preparation.
- Weave this new thread through at least five of the core beads below where you stopped working (in Figure 4.4, these are beads 1–5).
- After stitching through three of the five core beads, tie a simple overhand slip knot around the threads passing through these beads.
- Continue to bring your needle and thread up through the top two core beads (2 and 1 in figure 4.4).
- Leave a small tail (which you will cut off once the thread is secure) sticking out of the first core bead you stitch into.
- Both the new thread and the old thread will now be coming out of the top core bead (1 in figure 4.4), side by side. Tie the new thread to the old thread using a square knot.
- Take the old thread and weave down through the spiral beads of the final stitch. Cut it off to end it.
- Cut off the tail of the new thread
- Continue beading with the new thread.

Clasp
(see figure 4.5)

- At one end of the necklace, add a button with shank. To do this, pick up three seed beads, pass through the shank of the button, and pick up three more beads.

- Stitch back down into the top core bead, exiting from the fifth bead from the top.
- Pass back through the spiral beads, the top core bead, all the loop beads, and the button shank a second time.
- You can repeat this one more time if you can get your needle though all the beads.
- End your thread by tying several overhand knots around the core thread and weaving the end into a few more beads.

FINISHING

- At the opposite end of necklace, pick up enough beads to make a loop that fits over the button you have chosen.
- Stitch back down into the top core bead and repeat the directions shown in figure 4.5 to strengthen the loop.
- End the thread.

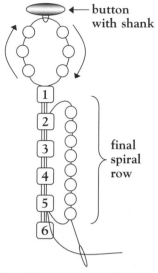

4.5. Adding button with shank for clasp.

MEDITATION
Bringing In the Light

Before you begin Project 8, I recommend taking time to do this chakra meditation. It will help you visualize bringing in the colors of the visible light spectrum in order to nourish and recharge your chakra system and thus your physical, emotional, mental, and spiritual body. (You can also use this meditation whenever you feel depleted in any region of your body, have injured yourself, or have developed an illness or disease. It will help you reenergize either the specific chakra that relates to the location of your problem, or your whole chakra system from bottom to top or top to bottom.)

1. Find a place and time to do this meditation where you will not be disturbed.
2. I suggest you do this meditation standing, but you can do it seated as well. If standing, have your feet about twelve inches apart, spine straight.
3. Take at least three deep breaths, relaxing your jaw, your shoulders, your stomach and any other place where you feel tension in your body on each exhalation.
4. Visualize your breath going to the base of your spine, down to your tailbone. Inhaling, feel each breath energizing your life force and feel your feet connected to the ground. Imagine a vortex of the color red spinning counterclockwise between your legs. Draw this deep red energy up from the earth until it completely fills your Root chakra with its pulsating vibrations. Feel this energy anchoring you deeply into the center of the earth as it activates the qualities of endurance, patience, stability, and structure within you. Let it envelop you with its heat and red-hot fire of creative potential. Take a deep breath and affirm your physicality and connection to the earth.
5. Bring your attention to your second chakra area, which is your pelvic region. Visualize your breath filling your belly, expanding your lower abdomen with each inhalation, releasing any tension held here with each exhalation. Imagine a vortex of the color orange spinning in a counterclockwise circle in front of your Sacral chakra. Bring this hot, orange, spinning energy into your pelvic region until it saturates you with its heat and fiery energy. Intensify the color orange as it expands your second chakra and allow it to flood you with the qualities of abundance, pleasure, and emotional well-being. Take a deep breath and affirm your center of personal creativity and physical balance.
6. Next, focus your attention on your third chakra, the area of your solar plexus. Breathe deeply into the region of your stomach, a place where you may hold tension and tightness. Allow the tightness to relax with each exhalation. Imagine a

vortex of brilliant yellow energy spinning counterclockwise in front of your solar plexus. Allow this fiery yellow ball of energy to warm your belly with its heat as it brings with it the gifts of self-worth, transformational willpower, and connection to your true feelings. Breathing deeply, affirm your center of personal power and self-identity.

7. Now, bring your focus to your forth chakra, located around your beautiful, pulsating heart. Allow your breath to fill your heart with ease and exhale, releasing the many burdens you have been carrying there. Imagine a vortex of radiant green light spinning counterclockwise in front of your heart. Bring this sweet, loving radiance into your heart and allow it to expand, filling you up with its green, vital energy. Let it bring you to a place of balance, peace, and harmony. With a deep breath, affirm your center of love, forgiveness, and compassion.

8. Visualize your breath filling your fifth chakra, in the region of your throat, releasing any tension you are holding here, especially in your jaw. Imagine a vortex of cerulean blue energy spinning counterclockwise in front of your throat. Allow the coolness of this blue color to flow into your throat, bringing you its gifts of self expression and the ability to speak your personal truth. Let this sky blue color fill you with its vitality as you bathe yourself in its luminescent color. Take another deep breath and affirm your center of creative expression and communication.

9. Bring your attention to your sixth chakra, located in the Third Eye center of your forehead. Use your breath to consciously relax your brow and any tension remaining there. Visualize a vortex of indigo blue color spinning counterclockwise in front of your Third Eye center. Bring the energy of this deep blue color into your sixth chakra, allowing it to fill you up with its liquid potentiality. This ray of blue light brings with it the gifts of discernment and spiritual awareness. Taking another deep breath, affirm your center of wisdom, imagination, and knowledge.

10. Finally, focus your attention at the top of your head, on your Crown chakra. Visualize opening this chakra by spinning it counterclockwise above you. Once open, imagine beautiful violet light flooding your Crown chakra with its radiance and allow this violet colored energy to flow through your entire being as if you're taking a bath in it. Let it reenergize you as it brings with it the gifts of spiritual love, bliss, harmony, and peace for you to embrace. This is your portal to the realm of Spirit. Taking a deep breath, affirm your center of enlightenment, transcendence, and your relationship with the Divine.

11. Give yourself permission to allow the inner peace and love you feel in this moment to be with you throughout your day. Any time you see one of the chakra colors reflected in the arena of your daily life, acknowledge its gift to your energy field with silent gratitude and appreciation.

PROJECT 8

Chakra Flower Sculpture

This project is a chakra mandala flower sculpture that has seven layers, each beaded in the color of a particular chakra. Every mandala flower is worked in flat circular gourd stitch; therefore, the instructions are the same for each layer. Before you begin each new layer, I recommend that you refer back to the place in the chapter where that specific chakra is described. Holding your focus on the attributes and characteristics for each particular chakra will help you ground the information more deeply into your consciousness. As you work in each color, you may find that it affects you in different ways. You may want to keep a journal nearby to write down your feelings and thoughts that surface as you work.

Chakra Flower Sculpture,
Wendy Ellsworth, 1997.
(For a color photograph of this project, see color plates 5a and 5b.)

If you are an advanced beader, you might want to place a gemstone cabochon in the center of each chakra flower and make a beaded bezel around it to hold it in place. Here is a list of suggested gemstones:

Chakra 1: ruby, bloodstone, hematite
Chakra 2: carnelian, tiger's eye, onyx
Chakra 3: topaz, amber, citrine
Chakra 4: rose quartz, diamond, green or watermelon tourmaline
Chakra 5: turquoise, blue agate, aquamarine
Chakra 6: sapphire, lapis lazuli, tanzanite
Chakra 7: amethyst, alexandrite

MATERIALS

- Seed beads, size 11, in each of the seven chakra colors, approximately 45 grams of each color

   Chakra 1: Root chakra—red
   Chakra 2: Sacral chakra—orange
   Chakra 3: Solar Plexus chakra—yellow
   Chakra 4: Heart chakra—green
   Chakra 5: Throat chakra—turquoise or cerulean blue
   Chakra 6: Third Eye chakra—indigo blue
   Chakra 7: Crown chakra—violet

- Silamide thread size A or Nymo thread size B, to match bead color of each layer
- Sharps short beading needles, size 12
- Synthetic wax
- Beading mat
- Scissors
- Ott light or desk lamp

PROJECT PREPARATION

- Pull off approximately 10 feet of thread and prestretch. If your bead holes are large enough, try working the thread doubled. If not, work it single width.
- Add the needle to the thread.

I have written out the directions for the first fourteen rows, and figure 4.6 shows a diagram of the thread path and beads for the first eight. After that, you are off on your own journey of exploration in beading and the Creative Spirit. Try it! You may be surprised at how much fun it is.

Row 1

- Pick up three beads and bring them down to the end of your thread, leaving a 6-inch tail. You can weave this tail into the sculpture after completing the first ten rows.
- Pass back through bead 1 a second time in the same direction and pull beads into a triangular shape.

Row 2

- Pick up two beads (beads 4 and 5 in figure 4.6), and stitch into bead 2 as shown in the diagram. Pick up two beads (beads 6 and 7) and stitch into bead 3.
- Pick up two beads (beads 8 and 9) and stitch into bead 1 *and* 4 and 5. (This is called a "step-up" and must be done at the end of *every* row to be in the correct position for the subsequent row. The step-up beads will always be the last bead of the previous row and the first bead of the row just completed. However, since the first stitch of row 2 is a two-bead stitch, you will pass through three beads for this initial step-up).
- Total = six beads (this refers to the total number of beads added in this row)

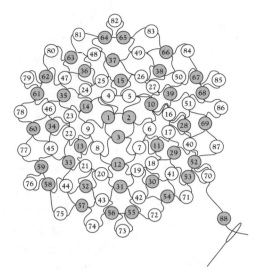

4.6. Flat circular gourd stitch, rows 1–8.

Row 3

- Place one bead between each bead of row 2. (Row 3 begins with bead 10 and ends with bead 15.)
- To end the row, stitch through beads 5 and 10 (the step-up).
- Total = six beads

Row 4

- Place two beads between each bead of row 3. (Row 4 begins with bead 16 and ends with bead 27.)
- Pass needle through beads 10 and 16 to end the row (the step-up).
- Total = twelve beads

Row 5

- Place one bead between each bead of row 4. (Row 5 begins with bead 28 and ends with bead 39.)
- Pass the needle through beads 16 and 28 to end the row (the step-up).
- Total = twelve beads

Row 6

- Place one bead between each bead of row 5. (Row 6 begins with bead 40 and ends with bead 51.)
- Pass the needle through beads 28 and 40 to end the row (the step-up).
- Total = twelve beads

Row 7

Work the row in the following sequence:

- Pick up two beads, take a stitch, pick up one bead, take a stitch. (Row 7 begins with bead 52 and ends with bead 69.)
- Repeat this sequence around the entire row.
- Pass the needle through beads 40 and 52 to end the row (the step-up).
- Total = eighteen beads

Row 8

- Place one bead between every bead of row 7. (Row 8 begins with bead 70 and ends with bead 87.)
- Pass the needle through beads 52 and 70 to end the row (the step-up).
- Total = eighteen beads

Row 9

- Place one bead between every bead of row 8. (Row 9 begins with bead 88.)
- Remember to step-up at the end of the row and every subsequent row.
- Total = eighteen beads

Row 10

Work the row in the following sequence:

- Pick up one bead, take a stitch.
- Pick up two beads, take a stitch.
- Pick up one bead, take a stitch.
- Pick up one bead, take a stitch.
- Pick up two beads, take a stitch.

- Pick up one bead, take a stitch.
- Pick up one bead, take a stitch.
- Repeat sequences 5–7 around the row.
- Total=twenty-four beads

Row 11
- Place one bead between every bead of row 10.
- Total = twenty-four beads

Row 12
- Place one bead between every bead of row 10.
- Total = twenty-four beads

Row 13
Work the row in the following sequence:
- Pick up one bead, take a stitch.
- Pick up one bead, take a stitch.
- Pick up two beads, take a stitch.
- Pick up one bead, take a stitch.
- Pick up one bead, take a stitch.
- Pick up one bead, take a stitch.
- Pick up two beads, take a stitch.
- Pick up one bead, take a stitch.
- Pick up one bead, take a stitch.
- Pick up one bead, take a stitch.
- Repeat sequences 7–10 around the row.
- Total = thirty beads

Row 14
- Place one bead between every bead of row 13.
- Total = thirty beads

Rows 15 and up
- Continue to work in a flat circular gourd stitch, increasing where there is a gap, and turning each two-bead increase into a radical increase in the subsequent row by inserting a single bead between the two beads.

- Try to keep your chakra flower as flat as possible. If you want to make it gently ruffle at the edges, make a series of two-bead increases in several rows. (Do not ruffle it too much because each chakra layer will be placed on the layer below to make your sculpture of seven chakra flowers.)

Final Row: Edging

Following are two possible edging techniques. The first is a simple three-bead picot stitch. To make this:

- Pick up three new beads and stitch into the next bead in the final row of gourd stitch.
- Repeat this three-bead picot stitch around the entire edge of your chakra flower. (See figure 4.7.)

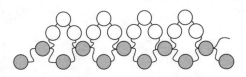

4.7. Three-bead picot.

The second is a five-bead edging stitch. To make this:

- Pick up four beads.
- Stitch back down through the third bead in the opposite direction.
- Pick up two beads and stitch into the next bead in the final row of gourd stitch.
- Repeat this five-bead edging stitch around the entire edge of your chakra flower. (See figure 4.8.)

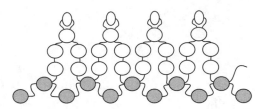

4.8. Five-bead edging.

◉ ◉ ◉

This completes the first chakra flower. Follow the same directions for creating each ascending chakra flower for the sculpture. You might want to make each flower ¼ inch smaller than the one below it, with your Root chakra flower measuring 4½ inches in diameter and your Crown chakra flower measuring about 3 inches in diameter.

When you have completed all seven layers of your chakra flowers, stack them in ascending order from Root to Crown. You have just created a mirror image of your own chakra system, in all its beauty and colorful majesty. Congratulations!

Shake Up Your Palette

Playing with Light and Color

The rainbow mirrors human aims and action.
Think, and more clearly wilt thou grasp it, seeing
Life is but Light in many-hued reflection.

—Goethe

Saturated with Color

We live in a world of light and color. And, oh, what a marvelous kaleidoscope of colors we are able to perceive! Just take a look around you right now. Can you mentally tally up all the colors you can see surrounding you, wherever you are? How many can you come up with?

Color permeates our lives; we are saturated with it. According to Barbara Ann Brennan, spiritual healer and best-selling author of *Hands of Light* and *Light Emerging,* it is our body's "life force." It tugs on the strings of our emotions and affects us on all levels of our being. Our eyes are the "windows of our souls," and it is through our eyes that we perceive the world in its entire color-filled splendor. Those of us who bead know how important color is to our work. Beading is an exercise in using color; every bead we pick up on our needle in order to take a stitch is a color choice we must make. For some, this choice comes naturally and easily; for others, color choices and combinations are difficult and sometimes frustrating.

I consider myself a color artist, with beads representing tiny photons of colored light that can be woven together to form infinite patterns of beauty and delight. My personal approach to color is an intuitive sense of what different color combinations feel like together in the moment of creating with them. For inspiration, I closely observe the color patterns found in nature during the four seasons of the year and often go for long walks in our forest in southeastern Pennsylvania or in the mountains of Colorado when I am fortunate enough to be there. Sometimes I might open a gardening book and wallow in the beautiful color combinations pictured there or the current issue of *Arizona Highways* magazine, which is always full of stunning photographs of that colorful desert state.

I think that the Creator must have a wonderful sense of humor when it comes to color. How could any of us have come up with the color combinations found on poisonous frogs or fungi? They are meant to catch our attention and warn us of danger. Have you ever seen giraffes in the wild? They can be standing very close to where you are, yet their camouflaged colors make them almost invisible. Flowers come in such a variety of color combinations that it staggers the imagination. How about butterflies? On a trip to Australia, I was privileged to see an absolutely magnificent blue Ulysses fluttering by in its native rainforest habitat. It was such a thrill! The colors in nature can be an amazing source of inspiration for all of us working with beads.

Imaginations of Light

There is a most interesting truth about light: it is always invisible. If there is no object onto which light can fall, we will see only darkness. We can see light only if it is reflected; we can never see the light itself. This is why beads "catch the light" and make it possible for us to see them in the first place.

In his book *Catching the Light,* professor of physics Arthur Zajonc entwines the history of light and mind and explains the various imaginations that great thinkers have brought to the concept of light. As he traces ideas from ancient Egypt to modern physics, we learn that light is truly a mystery. Even the modern quantum theory of light is unable to unearth the real nature and meaning of light. Light has been and remains an enigma and puzzlement to the brightest minds in the world, from Sir Isaac Newton to Albert Einstein. The bottom line is that we still do not know what light actually is.

As babies we have a formative period when we begin to see with our eyes, and our new vision brings us the gifts of intelligible light, color, and shape. But something more is going on; vision is more than just being able to see with a functioning physical organ. We must also develop a formative *visual imagination* that interprets what we see. According to Zajonc, in addition to an outer light and eye, sight requires an "inner light" that transforms raw sensation into meaningful perception. The light of the mind must combine with the light of nature to bring forth a world that is visible to our eyes. Without this inner light, we are functionally blind.

We need the light of our mind working in conjunction with the light that is reflected into our eyes to be able to comprehend what it is we are seeing. Yet even then, what we are seeing is really only an illusion. What we actually see are light waves being refracted off the rods and cones in the interior of our eyes' retinas.

What about the *spiritual imagination* of light? Is the cosmos, as meditation guru Paramahansa Yogananda instructed, a varied expression of one power—light—guided by divine intelligence? If we look to ancient Hindu and Buddhist teachings, we find a belief that every thought or idea originates in sound frequencies and manifests as patterns of light that give form to our material world. In these traditions, the practice of art is seen as a creative path to higher consciousness. It becomes an alchemical process of integrating spiritual consciousness with our hands that do the work and the materials we use to make our art. When we bring conscious awareness to our artwork, we evolve and replace our fragmented selves with wholeness in body, mind, and spirit through the process.

How do you feel when you quietly sit and bead? Do you sense a peacefulness that you are drawn to? Do you find yourself slowing down and becoming fully absorbed in the creative process? What does "en-light-enment" mean to you? Can you perceive that you can be transformed through your beadwork— that, through your beadwork, you can tap into a fountain of joy that is your birthright? You might want to take some time to think about these questions and your own responses to them before continuing to read.

Beads can and do catch the light in wondrous ways. They entice us with their beautiful colors and capture our full attention. Our fingers want to touch them, to pick them up, to weave them into textiles that seduce us with their tactile allure. Whether they are made from glass, metal, gemstones, or even plastic, beads capture the light for us, showing us their magical, mystical spectrum of color.

When we bead, we are experiencing light in all its prismatic radiance, and I believe we are also directly experiencing the Light of God, the Creator, or Great Mystery. One of my teachers once gave me this mantra: "There is no place that I can go where I can find more God than in this moment, *now*!" In other words, the Creator is present in everything, in every moment of our lives; the Creator is omnipresent. So it makes total sense to me that we can explore our relationship with this Divine Source through our beadwork, surrounded by all our colored beads that can rejuvenate us with their healing energy.

Color Energy

We are energy beings, receptive to color in all its forms. For instance, each of our chakras is a specific color, and when we look at the color that pertains to a specific chakra, it will "feed" that chakra with its light energy.

When we have an aversion to a particular color, it could be that it relates directly to a place in our bodies where we are holding old hurts and wounds in the form of stuck energy. Dr. Jacob Liberman, a pioneer in the therapeutic use of color and light in mind/body integration, writes in his book *Light, Medicine of the Future* that one of his most important clinical discoveries was that the colors to which people were unreceptive correlated almost 100 percent of the time with the portions of their bodies where they housed stress, developed disease, or had injured themselves.

As a beader, are there colors you dislike strongly? Could it be because a particular color is associated with something from your past that you have been ignoring or perhaps might be unconscious of? This is another way we can use our beads as a therapeutic process. You may not feel comfortable doing this work on your own, however. In that case, you may want to work with an art therapist or a person trained in syntonic optometry (ocular phototherapy) who can help you discover those places in yourself that you need to bring back into the light. If you are on the path of self-discovery, you can use your love of beads and their colors to help you on this journey. Later in the chapter I will list some of the colors we work with and their suggested healing characteristics so that you can begin to use them consciously in your beadwork.

Color Theory

Color is a form of "mirage," according to Carolyn Benesh, coeditor of *Ornament* magazine, in her article "Fashion in Colors." She refers to color as having a "phantasmic" quality because it really does not exist but rather is based on how light waves refract off of our eyes. Basically, when light is broken down (reflected and absorbed) into different wavelengths, we are able to perceive the colors of the rainbow. Have you ever held a prism up to the sunlight and observed the rainbow that appears from the opposite surface? It is like magic. Doesn't it also feel magical when you are surrounded by all your colors of beads and your mind can hardly contain itself with all your ideas of how to work with them?

Each color has its own particular reflective and absorptive qualities. When sunlight hits the surface of an object, all the light rays are absorbed and reflected according to the properties of the colors of the object. When the sunlight hits a blue bead, for example, the bead absorbs all the light rays, separates out the blue wave, and reflects it back into our eyes so we perceive the bead as being "blue" in color. The color we think we are seeing is actually a combination of light waves and atomic particles bouncing off the surface of the bead and then being refracted off the interior of our eyes.

Think about this for a few minutes.

The perception of color involves two centers of our brain. Identifying, differentiating, naming, and our aesthetic response to a particular color is a left-brain activity that takes place in the left hemisphere of our cortex. Our more intuitive, instinctual, and reflexive response to color is a right-hemisphere brain activity. Obviously, both hemispheric responses are important when it comes to understanding our perception of color. For some people, however, because of their left-hemisphere brain dominance, it is more difficult to access their intuitive right-brain response when working with color.

There are two main color theories that artists use to understand how colors work in relationship with one another. This is important to those of us who bead because combining bead colors can be tricky. The color theories are a left-brained approach to working with color, however, and I do not claim to be a master at using them since my sense of color combinations comes from a more right-brain, intuitive, felt sense deep inside me.

Four excellent books can help beaders gain a thorough understanding of color theory. Two are written by bead artist Margie Deeb: *The Beader's Guide to Color* and *The Beader's Color Palette*, both of which demonstrate the use of specific color combinations. Sandra Wallace, another bead artist, wrote *The Beader's Color Mixing Directory,* which has a large number of examples of different projects showing color mixing with beads. And fiber artist Deb Menz wrote *Color Works: The Crafter's Guide to Color,* which contains a wealth of information on the principles of color use in textile arts, including bead art. If you would like assistance with color theory, I highly recommend any or all of these helpful books.

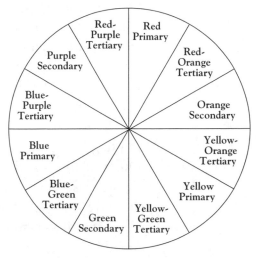

Color wheel: subtractive system of color.

The traditional artist's color wheel theory maintains that there are three primary colors: red, yellow, and blue. These are considered *primary* because they are pure and do not contain any other colors in them. *Secondary* colors are created by combining the primary colors with each other: red + yellow = orange, red + blue = violet, yellow + blue = green. Combining secondary colors with primary colors produces *tertiary* colors: red-orange, yellow-orange, yellow-green, blue-green, blue-purple (my favorite), and red-purple. This system is called a "subtractive" system of color because it is based on light that is reflected back from a surface and not absorbed by an object or other pigment.

The second color theory that artists use is known as the *additive* system. This system is based on light that is emitted from sources such as computer monitors, TV screens, or theatrical stage lights. In the additive spectrum of visible light, the

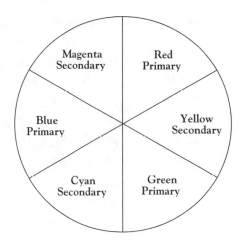

Color wheel: additive system of color.

primary colors are red, green, and blue. The light of these three colors when combined together produces white light. Combining any two of the three colors, again, produces secondary colors: red + green = yellow, red + blue = magenta, green + blue = cyan.

Choosing Colors

The greater or lesser impact of color depends on a combination of its *hue* (its actual shade or color), its *tonal value* (how light or dark it is), and its *saturation* (how bright or dull the color is). Colors can be warm (think of reds, oranges, and yellows) or cool (think of blues and purples). Warm colors tend to dominate when you use them in a bead design, while cool colors will recede into the background.

Because bead colors are so variable, they reflect light in varying degrees and are altered by the colors you place beside them. Other factors—such as thread color, ambient light, and surface finish—also create visual changes to the colors you combine in any given project. Margie Deeb suggests in *The Beader's Guide to Color* that if you want to predict how different beads will work together, it is best to weave up a sample swatch. But even then, the colors may look different when you work with them in your actual project.

I remember a student who asked me at least a half dozen times what color combinations I thought she should use in her project. She had different color combinations of the beads stacked up on straight pins, while the piece she was making lay nearby. My suggestion was to keep trying different beads on the piece itself to see how they looked because of all the variables that affect how bead colors appear.

This is how I work with color—I experiment. When I am ready for a color transition in one of my SeaForm sculptures, for example, I try a number of colors of beads on the piece itself to determine what feels right to me. Sometimes I might try ten or twenty different bead colors before I find the one I feel will work best. I create my own roadmap as I bead along, not necessarily knowing the destination but enjoying the journey one bead at a time. This is a reflection of my need for spontaneity and improvisation in my life as well as in my bead art. "Experiment! Explore! Enjoy!" has become my beading motto.

Surface Finishes on Glass Seed Beads

Glass seed beads have a large variety of surface finishes that affect how colors will interact and how our eyes will perceive them. *Opaque* seed beads have a flat finish and light will not pass through them. This was the first type of bead I used in my beaded mandalas as that was the bead primarily available from the Western Trading Post in Denver where I bought my supplies. All the tribal peoples of Kenya who do beadwork continue to use this type of bead in their traditional crafts.

Transparent seed beads allow light to pass through them, and thread color will change their hue substantially. I have used many transparent beads in my SeaForm series, and when they are backlit for photographic purposes, their colors are breathtakingly beautiful.

Opaque or transparent beads that have been etched to produce a nonreflective finish are called *matte* beads. You can actually matte your own beads by purchasing an etching substance and soaking the beads in it overnight.

Beads that have a rainbow coating on them are referred to as *Iris* or *Aurora Borealis (AB)*. These are some of my favorite seed beads as they are truly iridescent and add depth to bead projects.

Lined seed beads have silver, gold, or other colors lining the inside of the bead. A transparent bead might have an opaque color inside of it, which gives the bead a greater sense of depth. I have found that some of the colors lining transparent beads tend to fade when exposed to light. To check for this, place the beads beside a bright window for a few weeks. Also, the silver lining inside some beads can wear away with time, so you might not want to put them in a piece of jewelry that will be worn against the skin.

Opaque luster beads have a finish that is like a mother-of-pearl coating on them and are often used in a pastel palette. *Ceylon luster* beads have a translucent surface coating on them and blend well with other bead colors.

Galvanized beads have a surface finish that will often rub off quickly, though there is a new galvanized Japanese bead that has recently come on the market that the manufacturers promise will hold its finish. *Metallic* beads have a coating of real metal on the surface that will not rub off. These beads provide a wonderful rich contrast within a color palette, and I especially like using metallic beads with 22-karat gold for a special touch of elegance.

Each of these surface finishes plays a major role when you are choosing a color palette to work with. When you purchase beads, I hope you can either go to your local bead store or to a trade show where you can see and hold the beads in your hands. If the shop or show has fluorescent lights, the colors will not be "true" as you examine them, but if you can take them over to a window, you will be able to see their true color by the natural light. I have a difficult time ordering beads out of a catalog or from a website because it is hard to know what a bead's real color is unless I already know the bead and its stock number.

When working with bead colors, people tend to get stuck in their comfort zone. They often choose the same colors over and over again, and after a while their pieces tend to look like variations on the same color theme. Over the years a number of students have asked my advice on how to break out of this pattern, and I finally came up with a class titled "Shake Up Your Palette." I have modified the lessons from this class for an exercise that appears later in this chapter, and I hope you can do it with a beading pal or with a group of beading friends to help you broaden your color choices.

The Healing Qualities of Colors

In theory, every color has healing qualities associated with it that will affect us on many levels—physically, emotionally, and spiritually. Barbara Ann Brennan, in her book *Light Emerging: The Journey of Personal Healing,* discusses how color is essential to our health. She believes that our bodies respond to color through the chakra system as well as through the colors of the foods we eat, the clothes we wear, and the colors we use to decorate our living spaces.

Sitting in our work space, surrounded by all the colors of the beads we have chosen to work with, we are stimulating and nourishing ourselves with color on all these levels.

As light reflects off the bead surfaces, it enters those portions of our brain called the hypothalamus, the pituitary, and the pineal. The stimulation of these light-sensitive centers has an immediate effect on our physical, emotional, and mental state, depending on how we interpret the colors and what emotions we associate with them. Our response to the colors of our beads is personal and, most likely, predictably consistent. If we have a strong negative response to a particular color, it might relate to an old unresolved emotional issue that gets triggered when we see that color. It may also correspond to a chakra center in our body where we are holding stress or perhaps have developed a debilitating illness or injury. We can use these as clues in our path of self-development.

Over the years I have been interested in how color can be used as a healing tool and have investigated many different sources for information on the therapeutic use of color. Drawing on these sources, I have compiled some information on certain colors and the healing, spiritual qualities attributed to them. Please remember that this information is theoretical and is only meant to be a guideline. I offer these characteristics of colors as suggestions about how you might use color as a therapeutic tool in your beadwork. (If you are interested in gaining a deeper knowledge of these characteristics, I recommend reading the following authors' books: Barbara Ann Brennan, *Light Emerging;* Ted Andrews, *How to Heal with Color;* and Linda Clark, *The Ancient Art of Color Therapy.*)

Remember that how people respond to color is subjective, so while a color may mean one thing to one person, it may have an entirely different meaning for you. The key is how you *feel* when you focus on a particular color and bring it into your energy field. Questions to ask yourself include: How do I feel when I see this color? Do I have a strong negative or positive reaction to it? If so, can I remember what might have triggered this response from my past? Do I feel energized by this color? Do I feel excited, calm, peaceful, or happy when I see it? Do I feel repulsed or tense when I see it? How you feel about the colors you work with (or do not work with) in your beadwork are keys to opening doors to your own sacred center, not anyone else's.

Gold

Golden light has an extremely high frequency and is associated with our connection to God or Spirit. It helps connect us to our spiritual purpose and higher mind, grounding us in our personal power. It can strengthen every part of our body, mind, and soul. If we feel the need for protection, we can visualize surrounding ourselves with golden light. Painters have often placed golden halos around the heads of venerated saints and holy men and women from the past. Gold rings are symbols of the sacred bonds that unite us in marriage.

White

White contains the whole light spectrum within it. It helps connect us to our purity, increases our connection to Spirit, and strengthens our connection to others on the spiritual level. It can cleanse and purify our entire energy system and awaken great creativity within us. White light can also be used to surround ourselves and our loved ones in a cocoon of protection and love.

Silver

Silver can be used to help us discover and apply our creative imagination. It activates our innate intuition. Silver also has a very high frequency and helps energize us. It can assist us in being able to communicate more clearly. "Every cloud has a silver lining" is a saying that captures the healing qualities of silver.

Personal Mandala [1b]
Wendy Ellsworth, 1989

33"h x 10½"w

Glass seed beads, thread, leather, embroidery hoop, feathers, charms.

Geometric Mandalas [1a]
Wendy Ellsworth, 1993

11"h x 11"w

Glass seed beads, thread, leather, turned wooden discs.

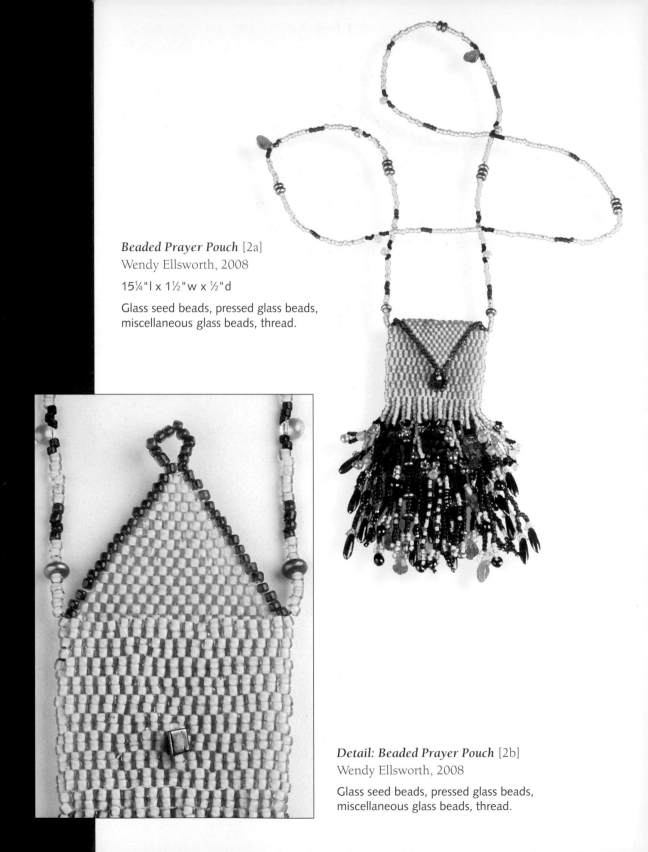

Beaded Prayer Pouch [2a]
Wendy Ellsworth, 2008

15¼"l x 1½"w x ½"d

Glass seed beads, pressed glass beads,
miscellaneous glass beads, thread.

Detail: Beaded Prayer Pouch [2b]
Wendy Ellsworth, 2008

Glass seed beads, pressed glass beads,
miscellaneous glass beads, thread.

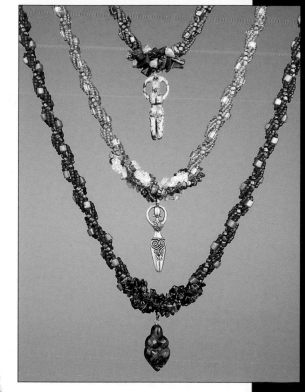

Goddess Archetype Necklaces [3b]
Wendy Ellsworth, 2008

12–13"l x ½"w x ½"d

Glass seed beads, glass cube beads, turquoise, sodalite, lapis lazuli, amethyst, fluorite, solite gemstone chips, thread. Goddess figurines: turquoise, sodalite, brass.

Prayer Beads for Barack Obama [3a]
Wendy Ellsworth, 2008

40"l x ½"w

African trade beads, antique silver beads, Raku, turquoise, metal, shell beads, miscellaneous glass beads, synthetic sinew.

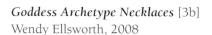

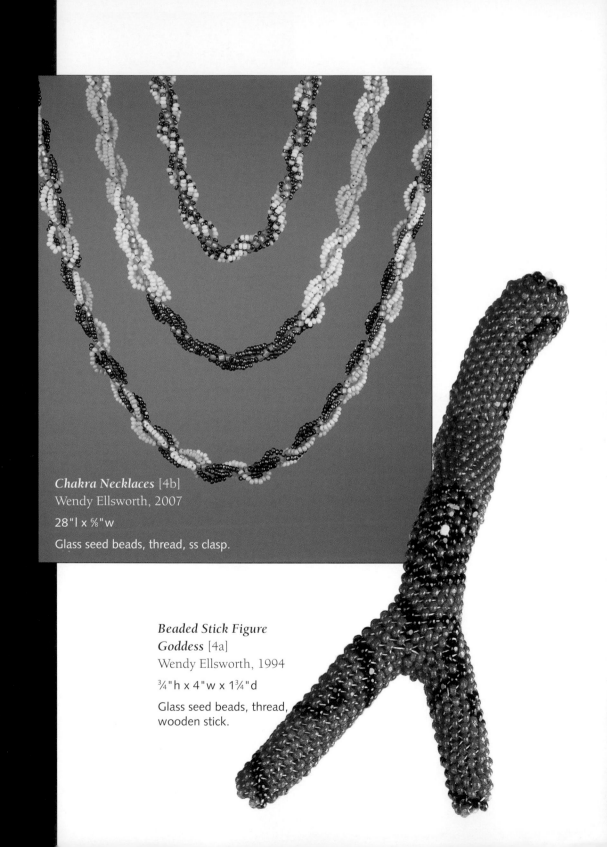

Chakra Necklaces [4b]
Wendy Ellsworth, 2007

28"l x ⅝"w

Glass seed beads, thread, ss clasp.

Beaded Stick Figure
Goddess [4a]
Wendy Ellsworth, 1994

¾"h x 4"w x 1¾"d

Glass seed beads, thread,
wooden stick.

Chakra Flower Sculpture [5a]
Wendy Ellsworth, 1997

4½"h x 4½"w x 4½"d

Glass seed beads, thread.
Cabochons: amethyst, coral,
cut glass, lapis lazuli, malachite,
Mexican opal, turquoise.

Chakra Flower Sculpture [5b]
Wendy Ellsworth, 1997

Glass seed beads, thread.
Cabochons: amethyst, coral,
cut glass, lapis lazuli, malachite,
Mexican opal, turquoise.

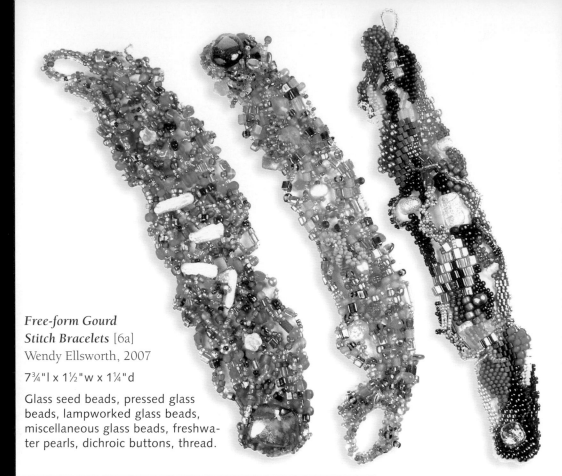

Free-form Gourd Stitch Bracelets [6a]
Wendy Ellsworth, 2007

7¾"l x 1½"w x 1¼"d

Glass seed beads, pressed glass beads, lampworked glass beads, miscellaneous glass beads, freshwater pearls, dichroic buttons, thread.

Ruffled Cabochon Brooches [6b]

Wendy Ellsworth, 1998

½"h x 2"w x 2"d

Glass seed beads, gemstone chips, miscellaneous glass beads, thread, Ultrasuede, pinback. Cabochons: crinoid, sugalite, opal, jasper, gold-stone.

Dutch Spiral Necklaces [7a]
Wendy Ellsworth, 2007

21"l x ⅜"w

Glass seed beads, thread.

Spiral Vessels [7b]
Wendy Ellsworth, 2001

5¼"h x 2¼"w x 2½"d, 2¾"h x 2¼"w x 2¼"d

Glass seed beads, 4 mm cube beads, thread.

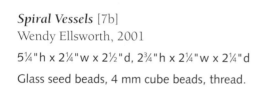

Song Beads [8a]
Wendy Ellsworth, 2009
2"l x ½"w x ½"d
Glass seed beads, thread.

Herringbone Stitch Cuffs with Freshwater Pearls [8b], Wendy Ellsworth, 2008
7¾"l x 2"w x ½"d
Glass seed beads, freshwater pearls, thread, dichroic buttons.

Violet

Violet can help us balance our spiritual and physical energies. It is the color of the Crown chakra and of our cosmic awareness. It can also act to shield us from negativity and help protect us in our spiritual journey. Violet is known for its antiseptic qualities and its potential for soothing pain and relieving tension in our physical bodies. It can be used to stimulate inspiration and humility. Balanced with yellow, it can help a person with a fragile ego regain a sense of self-identity. It is referred to as a royal color because it used to be reserved only for royalty.

Indigo

Indigo is the color of the Third Eye chakra and the color of universal healing. It can help bring our awareness to a higher plane by opening our consciousness to what is limitless and expansive, helping us connect to the deeper mysteries of spiritual life. Visualizing indigo raises our vibration to a higher frequency. It can help bring us clarity as an antidote to feelings of anger and frustration. It can also connect us to our sense of purpose as well as open us to deeper spiritual perception and feelings of ecstasy, devotion, and intuition. Because indigo is a cool color, it might need to be counterbalanced with yellow or orange.

Blue

Sky blue, turquoise, and cyan are all colors of the Throat chakra. They can bring a sense of peace and tranquility to our energy field and help soothe hyperactivity. They can also help stimulate our creative expression. All shades of blue are cool colors with strong healing potential and can soothe inflammation on any level. If we are feeling stressed out, the color blue can calm us.

Green

The color of the Heart chakra, green can help bring balance into our lives, soothing our nerves and reenergizing us if we are feeling depressed or fatigued. It is the predominant color in nature, propelling us toward growth, change, and transformation. Green is widely used in healing therapies, especially for inflamed conditions of the body. It can revitalize us on all levels, uplifting our spirit and restoring harmony to our physical body. Focusing on the beautiful green spectrum can help ease our feelings of emotional pain, loneliness, and jealousy. It can also be used to awaken hope, faith, and peace in us and in others. The combination of green with rosy pink is the color of kindness and compassion; watermelon tourmaline is the perfect example of this harmonious relationship.

Rosy Pink

According to Rosicrucians, rosy pink is the color of universal love. They believe that by visualizing this color for yourself and others, universal love will become manifested in body, mind, and spirit. Rosy pink can be used to awaken compassion, love, and purity within ourselves. It is an essential color for the Heart chakra.

Yellow

Yellow is the color of the Solar Plexus chakra. It can stimulate the mind and nervous system and help reawaken an enthusiasm for life, which makes it a useful color to help with feelings of depression. Yellow is a happy, joyful color, the color of contentment and confidence. It can help us create a positive mental framework so that we can digest new ideas. Too much yellow can be balanced with violet, its complementary color, in order to calm our Solar Plexus chakra region.

Orange

The color of our Sacral chakra, orange charges our sexual energy and enhances our immune system. A hot color, orange is full of vital energy and deeply connected with our life force, our joy, and our passion. It can stimulate feelings of sociability as well as our appetite. It can also increase our ambition and reflect feelings of confidence and strength. Orange can help lift us out of depression and is a good tonic for the soul. A blast of orange in our beadwork will automatically catch the eye and draw attention to our work.

Red

Red is the color of the Root chakra and has the longest wavelength in the color spectrum. It is the color of our life force and connects us to the energy of the earth. It gives strength to our will to live in the physical world. It can be used to signify danger, poison, or a threat, and is sometimes used as a protective barrier to keep others away. It can also be used as a signal of assertion and self-confidence. Red catches our attention in positive and negative ways. It can stimulate our deepest passions, such as sex and love, or feelings of hatred and revenge.

Brown

Brown enhances a rich connection to the earth and helps ground us energetically. It can be especially effective for emotional and mental disturbances, helping to bring us gently back to ourselves. It can help awaken common sense and discrimination and is a good color for those of us who need to work on creating healthy boundaries with others. If we are feeling "spacey," it can also help bring us back "down to earth."

Black

Black contains the entire color spectrum and can help us draw within and stay centered. It is a supportive and nurturing color. It can help us enter into deep internal creative forces by bringing us into the mysterious void, the source of unmanifested life waiting to be born. A protective color, black can be used to ground and calm ourselves if we are extremely sensitive to external stimulation. Too much black, however, can contribute to feelings of depression; it is best used with another color where it will highlight and increase the other color's visibility.

◉◉◉

These are examples of the healing characteristics of certain colors. When we are beading, we are constantly making choices about colors and color combinations. If we bring a higher level of awareness to how colors can affect us, we will not only be playing in the creative process but will have an opportunity to heal or nurture ourselves at the same time: a win-win situation. If we focus on creating beaded gifts for our friends who are ill or going through some form of crisis, we can knowingly choose colors that can help them with the affliction or challenge they are facing in their lives.

I believe that each step in conscious awareness leads us in the direction of wholeness and healing in our spiritual journey—and that includes our conscious choice of the colors in our beadwork. As we weave our beads with our hands, we are participating in an alchemical process, transforming these tiny objects into art—and transforming ourselves at the same time.

Exercise
Shake Up Your Palette

This exercise is a modification of a class I have designed for beading students to help them break out of their pattern of working within a narrow, limited range of colors. The exercise can be done alone, or you might want to share it with another beading pal or a group of beaders, perhaps members of your bead society, if you belong to one.

If you would like to do this with a friend or group, here is how to proceed:

1. Ask a friend or invite a group of people to participate. (You will need a place large enough so you can all work together at the same time.)

2. Decide ahead of time what project to make. It could be the first project for this chapter, the Free-form Gourd Stitch Bracelet or a spiral rope necklace. The project itself is not what is important; it is the focus on color. Ask each person to bring the supplies to make the project in their favorite color palette of beads.

3. Invite each person to put out their beading materials and spend the first half hour (or longer, depending on how many people are participating) getting the project started using their own beads.

4. At the end of the allotted time period, direct each person to get up and move one seat clockwise, leaving their beads and project behind. When they sit in the next place, they will have the opportunity to work on another person's piece in that person's favorite color palette.

5. Encourage each person to take a few minutes to look over the color choices and then jump in and get to work. It is important not to spend much time analyzing or being scared of making a "mistake" on someone else's piece. This is a right-brain exercise of being in the present moment and working with colors that might be outside of your comfort zone. It is in the *experience* of having to work in another color palette that will help you find the confidence to break out of your narrow use of colors.

6. Make sure each person gets to work on everyone else's piece. Then have everyone come back to their own piece and spend another half hour working on it.

7. At the end, have a group discussion about how each person felt about the experience.

This exercise of working with other people's color palettes is an excellent way to gain confidence with new colors. It can also be very freeing. You will find that other people have used your beads in ways you probably would not have thought of! It is a great way to stretch yourself and "shake up your palette."

If you choose to do this exercise by yourself, I suggest gathering together a color palette that is unlike any that you have worked in before and making a project of your choice using these new colors. Pay attention to how you feel as you are working with this different choice of colors. Here are some questions to ask yourself as you are working: Am I comfortable or uncomfortable working with this color palette? How big a stretch is this for me? Would I use this color combination again? Why or why not? Are any of these colors stirring up old memory associations? If so, what are they? How could I start to include these new colors in my work?

PROJECT 9
Free-form Gourd Stitch Bracelet

This is a fun project that will help you learn to work in free-form gourd stitch (also referred to as peyote stitch). I first encountered free-form gourd stitch through the work of Joyce J. Scott, who pioneered its use in her three-dimensional sculptural beadwork. Her hand-drawn cartoon book, *Fearless Beadwork: Handwriting and Drawings from Hell*, gives delightfully irreverent instructions on how to do the stitch in an improvisational manner. Bead artist Jeannette Cook followed Scott's light-hearted manual with her book *A Sculptural Peyote Projects Primer*, which gives instruction in how to use the stitch to make a number of fun projects. For this bracelet, you can use as many colors as you could possibly want and combine them in a single piece of jewelry

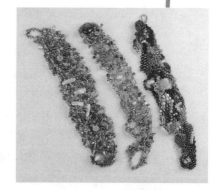

Free-form Gourd Stitch Bracelets,
Wendy Ellsworth, 2007.
(For a color photograph of this
project, see color plate 6a.)

MATERIALS

- Beads in multiple colors, sizes, shapes, and textures: sizes 11 to 6 seed beads, 4-millimeter cube beads, hex beads, triangle beads, teardrops, fire-polished beads, pressed-glass beads, pearls, larger focal beads, lampworked beads, etc. (*Hint:* choose a specific color palette to work in, or let your project be a total fiesta of color choices.)
- Button with a shank or clasp of your choice
- Silamide thread size A or Nymo size B (to match your predominant bead color)
- Sharps short beading needles, size 12 (or your own preference)
- Scissors

- Beading mat
- Ott light or desk lamp

PROJECT PREPARATION

- Pull off approximately 9 feet of thread and prestretch it by pulling it out between your hands, working your way along its entire length.
- Add your needle onto the thread and bring it to the middle, so you are working with a double thread.
- Pick up a bead with a large hole, perhaps a size 6 or E bead, and bring it down to the ends of your thread, leaving approximately a 6- to 8-inch tail.
- Pass your needle back through the bead two more times, being careful not to stitch into the thread. This bead will be a "stop" bead, preventing the first row of beads from falling off the end of the thread when you pick them up with your needle, and will be removed or woven in later. You can wax your thread to make it easier to work with.

Base Row (Rows 1 and 2)

- Pick up beads in random color segments, with around eight to twelve beads in any given color segment, running them down to the stop bead.
- Measure the length against your wrist; you want the length to be approximately ¼- to ½-inch shorter than your actual wrist measurement. This first line of beads becomes rows 1 and 2.
- *Note:* Try to use beads with larger holes at both ends of the bracelet since you will be stitching through them multiple times. Do not pick up any really large beads in this base row.

Row 3

- Make a turn: Pick up two more beads and stitch back into the fourth bead from the end. (In figure 5.1, this is shown as bead 15.) You are now going to bead in the opposite direction.

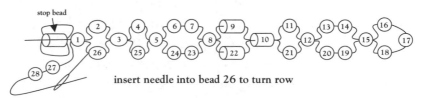

5.1. Making the turn at the end of base row.

- Work your way back along the original line of beads by picking up a new bead, skipping over a bead in the original line, and stitching into the next bead in the original sequence.
- You can start to make larger gaps by picking up two or three new beads, skipping two or three beads, and stitching into one, two, or three beads. (Figure 5.2 shows how to do this.)
- As you get to the different sizes and colors of beads in your base row, just add new bead(s) in those same sizes and colors.
- You can begin to blend colors by choosing bead colors that extend the color of your base row into the row you are adding.
- At the end of row 3, pick up two beads (beads 27 and 28 in figure 5.2) before turning and starting row 4. If there is an extra bead at the end of your base row, skip it for now. You can remove it when you take off the stop bead. (Figure 5.2 shows stitching into bead 26 in order to be in position to begin row 4.)

Row 4

1. Pick up a new bead (bead 29 in figure 5.3), and stitch into the next bead sticking down in row 3 (bead 25).

5.2. Making the turn at the end of row 3.

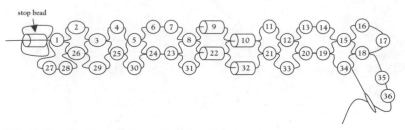

5.3. Making the turn at the end of row 4.

2. Continue to pick up a new bead or beads and stitch into the next bead sticking down in row 3. You are filling in the gaps that were created in row 3. You are now working in gourd stitch.

3. Pick up two beads to make the turn at the end of the row (beads 35 and 36 in figure 5.3). If you pick up two beads at the end of each row, the outer edge will not be completely flat.

Rows 5 and up

1. Repeat the directions in row 4 as you continue to work in gourd stitch, beading your way up and down the rows, adding in additional colors when desired. Remember this is "free-form" beading, so let loose and let the piece make itself.

2. You can work off both sides of the bracelet so that the base row becomes buried somewhere toward the center of the bracelet. When you have at least five rows completed, you can start to add "bridges" to create a three-dimensional effect.

BRIDGE

- To make a "bridge," pick up a number of beads of different colors, sizes, and shapes onto your needle, as you did in the base row. (In figure 5.4, the shaded beads form the "bridge.")
- Take your next stitch into a bead farther along in the row you are working on, skipping over a number of beads.
- Continue along the row, adding more bridges if you choose to. This is a good place to make a color transition by making the beads in your bridge a new color or colors.
- When you come back to the bridge in the subsequent row, begin to work off the beads in the bridge, not the beads in the

base of the bracelet. This will be a repeat of row 3, where you pick up a bead, skip a bead, and stitch into the next bead in sequence. (In figure 5.4, this is shown as the clear beads below the shaded beads.)

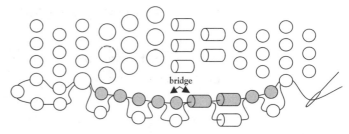

5.4. Gourd stitch bridge.

- Continue to bead the rows, adding bridges wherever and whenever you want.
- If the bracelet starts to curve, you can straighten out the curve. To do this, straighten the bracelet and see where it wants to curve upward. Start a new bridge that is slightly shorter than the upward curve. This will bring the bracelet back into shape.

ADDING THREAD

When adding a new thread, I suggest using the following method. The principle stays the same no matter what stitch you are working in.

- You need to stop working with the old thread and lay the project aside for the moment.
- Pull off approximately 9 feet of new thread and prestretch it by pulling it out between your hands, working your way along its entire length.
- Add your needle onto the thread and bring it to the middle, so you are working with a double thread.
- Weave this new thread into your project so that it ends up coming out of the same bead as the old thread, putting one or two slip knots around several threads along the way to secure it.
- Tie the new thread to the old thread with a square knot.
- Take the old thread and weave it through a few beads. You can put a slip knot around a thread to secure it. Cut it off to end it.
- Cut off the tail of the new thread and continue beading.

CLASP: BUTTON AND BEAD LOOP

Button

If you want to use a button with a shank, add it to one end of your bracelet as you are working on it, stitching through the shank several times as you go up and down your bracelet rows.Because you probably want it centered, you will need to decide when to add it while you are working on the piece.

Loop

If the bracelet is a bit tight on your wrist, you can extend it when you make the loop. I like to work the loop in several rows of gourd stitch so it is more interesting to look at.

- Pick up an even number of beads (number 1s in figure 5.5) and stitch back into the bracelet so that they form a loop that is large enough to fit around the button.
- Reverse direction and pick up a bead; skip a bead, and stitch into the next bead in the base row. (This is a repeat of row 3 for the bracelet and is shown as all the number 2s in figure 5.5.)
- Reverse direction again and place a bead between every number 2 bead in the loop (number 3s in figure 5.5).

FINISHING

- If you have not already removed the stop bead, do so now.
- Thread a needle onto one strand of thread and weave it carefully into your bracelet, knotting it as you would normally end a thread.
- Repeat with the second strand.

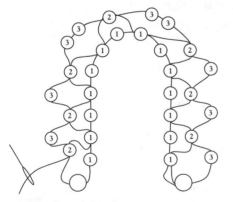

5.5. Gourd stitch loop.

◉⊙◎

Before beginning Project 10, I encourage you to use the following meditation to help you with choosing the bead colors for your design.

MEDITATION
Color

1. Sit in a chair with your feet flat on the floor and your back as straight as possible. Gently hold the cabochon you have chosen in one of your hands.
2. Close your eyes and take at least three deep breaths, releasing any tension you feel in your body.
3. Consciously relax your jaw, your shoulders, your belly.
4. Bring your attention to your Third Eye center between your eyebrows.
5. Visualize a clear white light emanating from this center and allow this healing light to flow into all parts of your body.
6. Bring your focus back to your Third Eye center and silently state your intention to make this project.
7. After stating your intention, visualize the cabochon you have chosen for your project. Feel it in your hand. If it is a natural stone, can you sense its energy field?
8. Focusing your attention on the cabochon, ask that the perfect colors of beads to use for the project be shown to you in your mind's eye.
9. Wait with patience for an answer to your request to come from Spirit.
10. When you have been shown the colors to use, offer your gratitude to Spirit for the guidance you have just been given.

11. When you feel the meditation is complete, open your eyes, and when you are ready, continue to gather the materials for your project.

Ruffled Cabochon Brooch

Many people have asked me to teach a one-day class on how to make one of my SeaForm sculptures. Because that would be impossible (it takes me many weeks to make a SeaForm), I came up with this small project that includes the principles of how I make my larger SeaForms. You may want to choose a special gemstone cabochon that pertains to a specific chakra (see the list in chapter 4, Project 8.)

Consider choosing your bead colors for their specific healing qualities, or making your brooch using the colors of the chakra system (two examples are shown on color plate 6b).

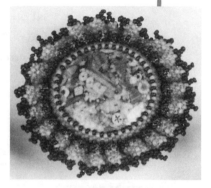

Crinoid Cabochon Brooch,
Wendy Ellsworth, 1998.
(For a color photograph of this
project in several versions,
see color plate 6b.)

MATERIALS

- Stone or glass cabochon (any size or shape)
- Leather or Ultrasuede for backing pieces
- Czech and Japanese seed beads (no Delicas), size 11, in three or more colors, at least 20 grams per color
  (See the important color suggestions in the instructions for the ruffle portion of this project.)
- Seed beads size 13 or 15, for final row of beaded bezel (you will only need a few of these)
- Silamide thread size A or Nymo size B, to match main bead color
- Sharps short beading needles, size 12
- Pin back to fit cabochon
- Multipurpose cement (Barge leather cement or Bond 527)
- Beading mat

- Scissors
- Leather punch or matte knife
- Ott light or desk lamp

PROJECT PREPARATION

- Place the cabochon on a small piece of leather or Ultrasuede. Mark around the cabochon with a pen, following its contour.
- Apply the multipurpose cement to the back of the cabochon and the surface of the leather inside the pen line. Let the glue set up for five minutes; then press the glued surfaces together.
- Cut out the leather around the cabochon about ⅛-inch from the edge (see figure 5.6). Be careful to leave enough leather to accommodate the width of the first row of beads. (*Note:* If the cabochon is small, cut the leather backing large enough to accommodate the length of the pin back.)

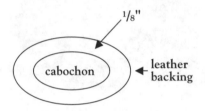

1/8"

cabochon

leather backing

5.6. Cutting out leather with cabochon attached.

- Place the cabochon and cut leather on the wrong side of a second piece of leather, trace around it, and cut it out. Reserve this piece for the backing of the brooch.

BEADED BEZEL (AROUND THE CABOCHON)

Base Row—Backstitch

- Thread a needle with about 36 inches of single thread. Tie two knots, one on top of the other at one end. (If you prefer to work with a double thread, do so after the first row.) I burn the tip of the thread to make a little ball beside the knot. If the ball sizzles up into the knot, start over.
- Pass the needle through the leather from back to front beside the cabochon. Work the first row in a circle around the outer perimeter of the cabochon in two-bead backstitch, using your size 11 beads (refer to chapter 1, Project 1, figure 1.1 for guidance).
- Continue around the base of the cabochon. When you get to the last stitch, you want to be able to fill the gap with two beads. If necessary, choose narrower or wider beads for the

last few stitches so that two beads will fit. Take a normal backstitch, but also continue through the first bead of the row a second time.

Row 1—Gourd Stitch

- Pick up a bead, skip the next bead on the base row, and stitch through the next bead (see figure 5.7).
- Continue working around the base row, picking up a bead *and* stitching through every other bead on the base row. Keep the tension very tight, and pull the new row of beads up onto the side of the cabochon.
- When you get to the end of the row, pass the needle through the first bead of the base row and the first bead of row 1 (called a "step-up"). (See figure 5.7: bead 30 is the final bead in row 1, and the final stitch is into beads 1 and 21.)

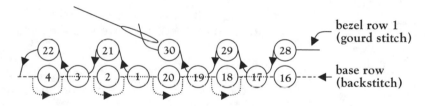

5.7. Gourd stitch bezel, row 1.

Row 2—Gourd Stitch

Depending on the size and shape of your cabochon, you will need to either work row 2 in regular gourd stitch, or you will need to do an even number of evenly spaced decreases. To work in regular gourd stitch:

- Pick up a single bead and stitch into the next bead sticking up from row 1.
- To decrease, pass your needle through the next bead in sequence without adding a bead (see chapter 3, Project 6, figure 3.10 for guidance).
- End the row the same way you ended row 2, with a step-up.

Row 3—Gourd Stitch

If you decreased in row 2, this row will be your final row. Follow the directions for row 4. If you did not already decrease, then row 3 will require an even number of decreases evenly spaced around the cabochon. To decrease:

- Pass your needle through the next bead in sequence without adding a bead (see Project 6, figure 3.10 for guidance).

Row 4—Gourd Stitch

Row 4 will be the final row.

- Substitute your size 13 or 15 beads for 11s in this row.
- When you get to the gap where you decreased in row 3 (or 2), you will probably need to put two beads to fill the gap.
- Go through all the beads of rows 3 and 4 again (without adding beads) to tighten and strengthen the edge of the bezel.
- Weave and tie off your thread into the beadwork.

PIN BACK

- Place the pin back above the midline on the right side of your second piece of leather.
  - Mark both ends of the pin back on the leather and punch small holes or cut small slits there.
  - Open the pin back and place the wrong side of the leather over it.
  - Push the pin through one hole and the catch through the other.
  - Apply cement to the back of the piece of leather with the cabochon and the wrong side of the second piece of leather plus the pin back.
  - Let the glue set up for approximately five minutes. Then press the two pieces together.

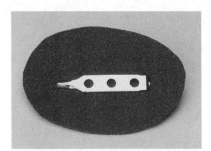

Ultrasuede, showing pinback placement.

RUFFLE

Here are a few important suggestions concerning the ruffle:

- Use three contrasting colors of beads (which I will refer to below as color 1, color 2, and color 3) to make rows 1–3 of the ruffle. If you use the same color bead, it will be extremely difficult to see which bead you need to stitch into once the ruffle has really started to undulate. Do not use black or cut beads if this is your first piece because they are very hard to see.
- When doing the two-bead stitches in the ruffle, pick through your beads and find thinner ones for each of these increases. This will make the increases less noticeable and create less of a gap.
- If the holes in the beads are large enough, you can work the thread doubled.
- To get started, weave a new thread into the beadwork bezel so that it exits one of the "down" beads (closest to the backing) of the base row (see figure 5.8).

Ruffle Row 1 (see figure 5.8)

- Pick up two beads in color 1 and stitch through the next "down" bead.
- Repeat all the way around the base row. Keep a tight tension on the thread. (Keep your tension even and tight and watch for your thread hooking itself around another bead as you take a stitch. Stop and check each and every stitch to prevent this from happening. Loose tension will result in huge gaps between beads in subsequent rows.)

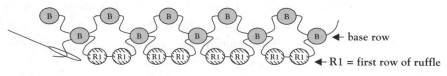

base row

R1 = first row of ruffle

5.8. Gourd stitch ruffle, row 1.

- After adding the last two beads of the row, stitch through the *first* base-row bead again *and* the *first* bead added in the first stitch of the row you have just completed (the step-up). Your thread will be coming out of the first bead of this two-bead stitch.

Ruffle Row 2 *(see figure 5.9)*

Here is the bead sequence for row 2:

- Pick up one bead in color 2, and stitch through the next bead in row 1; pick up two more beads in color 2, and stitch through the next bead in row 1.
- Repeat this sequence all the way around the row. Place each single bead stitch in the center of every two-bead stitch from row 1. Place the two-bead stitch in between each set of two beads from row 1.
- End row 2 by passing the needle through the first bead of row 1 and the first bead of row 2 (step-up).

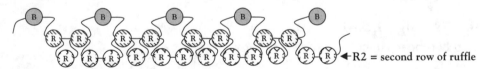

5.9. Gourd stitch ruffle, row 2.

Ruffle Row 3 *(see figure 5.10)*

- Pick up one bead each stitch in color 3, passing the needle through every bead of row 2. This is harder than it sounds. Figure 5.10 makes the process look flat, but the beadwork ruffles up and down. You will need to use extra care in determining which is the next bead in the row. A helpful hint is to remember that you are stitching into each color 2 bead from row 2.

5.10. Gourd stitch ruffle, row 3.

Ruffle Rows 4–12

- Continue to add one bead in each stitch around every row. If you want to make the brooch ruffle more, add two beads per stitch wherever you choose in the row.
- On the subsequent row, put a single bead between each two-bead increase, as on rows 2 and 3.

Edging

I like to use a simple edging technique called picot edging. All you need to do is to add three beads per stitch around the final row (see chapter 4, Project 8, figure 4.7 for guidance).

Dance with the Rhythm

6

Ten Tools of Creative Expression

Dance with the rhythms of creativity, don't sit on the sidelines seeking to control it.

—Matthew Fox

The Spirit of Creativity

Creativity is intrinsic to our lives. It is not something outside of us; rather, it is an innate spiritual force that lives within each of us. We are born with it, and as children we were completely filled with it. We did not have to think about being creative; we lived and breathed the Spirit of Creativity. We experienced its energetic force easily, before our left brains became dominant. Can you remember when you were young and how much fun it was to draw and paint, to sing and dance, to make up plays and stories with your overflowing imagination? Do you have children or grandchildren in whom you observe this creative energy alive and active?

Even if you do not feel that you are creative, that Spirit of Creativity still lives inside of you waiting to be reactivated. We *are* this force of Creative Spirit, and it is us. We cannot separate ourselves from it. However, we can suppress it to the point that we do not remember it has a permanent residence inside of us. Most of us were well trained in school to bury our creativity in order to learn to think analytically and recite what we were taught. Many of us were not encouraged to think for ourselves, to retain our spontaneity, our joie de vivre. Gradually, we learned to "stuff it" in order to fit into the cultural institutions that trained and employed us. Radical thinkers and artists are still shunned and feared specifically because they think and act outside the box that most people find themselves molded into.

People often tell me that they are not "creative," implying that only "artists" are immersed in creativity. This is absolutely not true! Each of us has within us the ability to open to the mystery and wonders of life and be able to express them in our own individual ways. When we express them, we are tapping into our creativity, no matter what form we chose for our outlet.

It is up to us to uncover, rediscover, and reconnect with this essence of creativity long buried. It lives in the right hemisphere of our magnificent brains, ready and willing to be reactivated. We need to get back to an internal balance within our brains that will allow us to dance with the rhythms of our creativity again. It is still there; we just need to allow the train of our imagination to travel down an old track that has not been used in a while. Our power of imagination can then join forces with divine creativity to reveal whatever it is that our amazing brain has thought up. It might be something beautiful, it might be something ugly, it might be something painful; whatever it is, we the makers are transformed in the process, discovering aspects of ourselves that have long been hidden or denied. It is this expression of Spirit that gives shape and value to what we have made.

In his book *Treasures of the Creative Spirit,* well-known artist and creative pathfinder Robert Piepenburg describes creativity as the reality presence of Spirit, a "primal transcendent force," without which we would be unable to give birth to new ideas and forms. It is the force though which we evolve naturally. Spirit flows through us as we create, and our mind, heart, and hands all work together to reveal the physical expression of this force. Piepenburg also poses that creativity is a *spiritual immersion* into ourselves, and this immersion creates a unity with Spirit.

What can stimulate us to remember our connection to this divine inner force? Any form of creative expression that we choose to indulge in has the possibility of linking us to it. The art we create with our beads is a direct expression of creativity. It is a response to our vision and our imagination, from which we extract ideas to help us make our art. Our beadwork can assist us in reconnecting with the Creative Spirit if we allow it, and through it we can understand ourselves at a deeper level. What we create with our beads can be a means through which we gain a new vision of self-awareness, leading us to a deeper level of spiritual meaning in our lives.

The next time you are beading, pay special attention to what you are aware of as you work. Is it thoughts of negativity or present moment spontaneity and joy? The more you consciously choose to use your beading moments for spiritual inspiration and self-development, the more you will be opening doors to this sacred connection and accessing your sacred center within.

Many of us have lost our connection to what is sacred. Yet it does not need to be this way. Many native peoples, for example, still experience this universal connection in a deep, life-fulfilling way. What has happened for the rest of us to sever this connection?

Jerry Mander, critic of technology and economic globalization, responds to this question in his stunningly relevant book *In the Absence of the Sacred.* He systematically shows how the evolution of modern technology has led us to an international, interconnected global web of political and technical entanglements that is unprecedented in its potential for negatively impacting all of our lives. Mander points out that the Industrial Revolution is not only *not* living up to its potential for creating human contentment, fulfillment, health, and world peace, it is actually creating terrible and possibly catastrophic impacts on the earth, as global warming and major climate changes are now showing us. We need to shift our priorities in order to come back into balance with the sacredness of life, and something as simple as weaving with little glass beads can be a way to achieve this.

Ten Tools of Creative Expression

Since the age of twenty-one, I have been on a conscious spiritual journey, and I have brought this spiritual awareness into my bead-work. When I intentionally connect with the Creative Spirit and allow it to flow through me, I feel the sacred connection to all forms of life. Over the years, I have identified some tools that help me use beading for spiritual inspiration and creative expression. I call this my "Tool Belt of Creative Expression." I hope these tools will help you develop the skills you need to reconnect with the Creative Spirit that resides within you.

1. Love

To love and to be loved is a primal need for everyone. Love is an energetic force, and I believe it is the foundation of creative expression. If you look at the Tool Belt of Creative Expression, you will see that I have placed love in the center. I would even go so far as to say that the tool belt itself is made out of love, since love is a necessary aspect of each and every other tool of creative expression. Love connects us to everything else in life, and without it, life becomes meaningless and empty. If love is absent in us, the makers, our creative projects will be void of true value and spiritual substance. There is a direct causal relationship between the two. When love is the foundation of our creative expression, the things we make with our beads will be infused with transformative energy. All forms of energy

Tool Belt of Creative Expression.

have a vibration that can be sensed, felt, and sometimes even seen with our eyes, which means that an object made with love vibrates with the frequency of love. Our beadwork is no exception.

When you bead with love, you open a doorway to your sacred center. Love is the key that unlocks the door. Once grounded in this hallowed place, your beading can become a bridge that can link you directly to the divine realm of the Creative Spirit. The next time you sit down to work on a beading project, consciously open your heart to love before you begin. See if you can notice a difference in how you feel while beading. Do you feel a greater connection to the Spirit of Creativity when your hands are infusing your creation with love?

2. Compassion

When love is the foundation of our creative expression, we can then learn to be open to the energy of compassion. I define "compassion" as the ability to embrace all things with unconditional acceptance and trust, which involves the qualities of our thoughts, emotions, and feelings. For Buddhists, compassion is the most important practice within their religion and is based on the realization that all things are interconnected.

While beading, we can learn to use these qualities of compassion as links to the Creative Spirit. Because beading is a present-moment activity, we can use it to become more aware of our thoughts while we are working. We can replace negative thoughts with more positive ones as we strive to embrace what is happening in our life with the acceptance that there is meaning and purpose in everything, that we are part of the quantum hologram or field that connects us to all that exists.

Compassion is another portal that can lead you to your sacred center. Practicing compassion will have a direct positive impact on your level of creativity. As you are beading, make a conscious effort to stay present with your thoughts, and notice when negative ones arise. As soon as you become conscious of a negative thought, shift it to a positive one. Have compassion for yourself as you do this inner work. Can you embrace all the parts of yourself, even the parts you might judge as less than perfect? Compassion can lead you to that place where you learn that there is "perfection" within imperfection. Adding compassion to your Tool Belt of Creative Expression can bring about an enormous shift in your attitude toward your beading as you begin to trust in the perfection that each moment brings, bead by bead.

3. Trust

Trust is a cornerstone in our lives—and in the creative process, as well. Trust gives us the courage to walk into the unknown as we labor to birth our ideas into physical reality. Trust is what allows us to walk to the edge of the cliff and jump off into the abyss. It is

what supports us when we work through a dark night of the soul. With trust as an ally, we find the confidence to handle life's many surprises and its multiple twists and bends.

When we sit down to bead, we need to draw on trust within ourselves for support in our beading efforts. Ironically, trusting the power of the creative process—even if we do not think of ourselves as "creative"—will increase the possibility of being creative.

When we do not know what color bead to use next or what shape to create, if we can trust that we will resolve these issues with experimentation and trial and error, we can move forward. If we trust the guide inside of us, we will know what to do.

I highly recommend that you try working free-form with different beading techniques as an exercise in letting go of control and jumping into the unknown, trusting that whatever you make will show you things you have not thought of before. Letting go and trusting that the universe will always not only support you but guide you is a major life lesson, and a valuable tool of creative expression.

4. Self-Confidence

Self-confidence generates creativity and is a gift of positive empowerment. It is a primal healing force that can expand our creative energies and our connection to the Creative Spirit. Self-confidence is crucial to being able to play in our creativity; it can take our art to places we have never gone before. Self-confidence helps us believe in our ability to push ahead with our ideas and manifest them into reality, and we need this in order to achieve our creative goals.

When we bead with self-confidence, we have a *knowing* that we will be able to achieve the creative aims we set for ourselves. Or, at the very least, we will have the self-confidence to know that if we encounter an obstacle, we will be able to find a way to deal with it. We will have the confidence in ourselves to find the right stitching technique, the right beads, or the right armature to complete our project. Used in this way, self-confidence is an essential tool of creative expression.

Your thoughts and your feelings are key players in using self-confidence to expand your creativity. Practice beading with self-confidence and notice if there is a difference in how you feel creatively. Trust yourself to be able to figure out the rhythm of a new stitch and use that self-confidence to work through the instructions until you get their rhythm imprinted into your tactile memory bank. Using self-confidence as a tool of creative expression will allow you to expand into any level of beading creativity you can possibly imagine and is yet another entrance into your sacred center.

5. Courage

Creativity takes courage. It takes courage to plunge into the unknown and sit in the darkness for a while. It takes courage to start a project not knowing what the end result will be or how it will be received. It takes courage to keep pushing until we understand

the "bigger picture" and get to that place of being able to say, "Aha!" It takes courage to present innovative ideas and new directions in our art forms, especially when tackling sensitive subjects.

Courage allows artists to make giant leaps in their creativity. We might call these "leaps of faith." Such leaps open gateways to new levels of exploration and can generate excitement that continues to fuel the creative process. New ways of approaching old ideas can lead to innovative techniques and tools, which in turn continue this dynamic, creative expression.

Sometimes it takes courage to tell your family that you need time to bead and to please leave you alone while you are working. Beading can be a "time out" for you, and if you have the courage to insist on taking it, you will be all the better for it. If you love yourself and trust that your need to create with beads is genuine and compelling, you can draw on courage combined with confidence to bead without fearing the consequences. Courage can give you the freedom to *be* and to *bead* with passionate delight.

6. Imagination

Whether we are conscious of it or not, each of us is endowed with a limitless supply of imagination, which is another cornerstone of our creative expression. We cannot be creative without it. Opening the doors to our imagination sets creativity into motion.

Imagination is also a vital component of spiritual and aesthetic growth that allows us to appreciate beauty and the wonderment of life. Imagination is a voice from within the depth of our souls to which we need to pay close attention. Listening to the voice of our imagination is a key to accessing the Creative Spirit. What we can imagine, we can attempt to create with our little glass beads. Give the same assignment and materials to ten different beaders, and the result will be ten very different interpretations. This is because each of us will use our own wonderful imagination as we work out the theme, and the result will be a unique, individuated work of art.

Beading is a wonderful way to explore your endless imagination. Once you have mastered a few of the main beading techniques and have some confidence in your beading skills, then you are ready to draw on your imagination for ideas to play with to create an original work. You might first sketch your ideas out on paper to get a basic idea of the image you want to make, then choose the beads you want to work with, and finally get to work. Keep asking yourself the question "What happens if...?" and see where it leads you. You are off on a creative journey, one bead at a time, into the unknown realm of the imagination. Have fun and enjoy the ride!

7. *Play*

Play is the free spirit of exploration. As adults, we tend to get very serious about life. All that seriousness leaves little time for play, and we all need more of it. When we make a conscious decision to restore play to its rightful place in our daily/weekly/monthly activities, playing can free us up and reestablish a direct connection to our imagination, which in turn will stimulate our creative juices.

Do you have children or grandchildren with whom you can get down on the floor and play? They are wonderful teachers to learn from and can remind us of how play increases creativity. Their imaginations are usually vivid and free and can remind us how we once used to be. They can help us reconnect with our Inner Child archetype. Playing with children can be a freeing, right-brain activity that counteracts our tendency toward left-brain dominance.

Playing with your beads can help you develop creatively. When you play with combining beading techniques in ways you have not done before, it can stimulate your imagination to come up with new ideas that you might want to create someday. (Keep what you make as sample references for future work.) Try playing with different color combinations to see how they interact with one another. Use this playtime to connect with the expression of your creative energy in ways that you normally would not give yourself permission to and you will be richly rewarded for your efforts.

8. *Joy*

Joy is an integral aspect of creative expression. Being joyful is a creative act in and of itself. Joy is a cornerstone in the foundation of our life's experience, a birthright that is freely available to each of us. In his book *Creativity,* religious-spiritual teacher Matthew Fox refers to joy as far more than the emotion that comes with  heightened consciousness or the mood that accompanies the experience of actualizing our own potentialities. He insists that when we experience joy as an aspect of the creative process, we are actually having a direct experience of the Divine. This joy is a deep, heartfelt experience of present-moment ecstasy, referred to by mystics as the *via positiva.*

I believe that when we bead, we can connect with this divine joy. As we bead, this joy fills us and becomes a pathway that can lead us directly to the Creative Spirit.

If you are having trouble finding joy as you bead, ask yourself what opens you to the state of joy? Dancing? Singing? A walk in nature? A swim in the ocean? Picture yourself doing what you love. Even brief glimpses of joy can remind you what it feels like to be in a state of joy and open the doors to more joy. If you can be fully present to the experience of joy, a deep sense of aliveness can flow into you. Through this aliveness you can connect with the Spirit of Creativity within you. "O bead joyful" is a phrase that you can use to remind you of this important tool of creative expression.

9. Intention

Intention is another tool of creative expression. When we set an intention for ourselves, it becomes like a wave of creative energy that we get to ride as we bring our intention into reality.

You can set an intention simply by saying to yourself, "It is my intention to … " (fill in the blank). There are some caveats to this process. Your intention needs to be dynamic, pointing to an activity that will connect you to the sacred within others and with all of life. (Otherwise it will just be an egoic exercise.) After stating your intention, you need to be open so that the energy set into motion can flow through you. If you state your intention with clarity before you begin a piece of beadwork, there will be a flow to your work that can make your beading a more creative process.

Start by sitting quietly before picking up your needle and bring yourself into the present moment. You may want to close your eyes. Then state your intention and feel it moving through you and out into the universe. Your intention can be as simple as saying, "It's my intention to play in the creative process with my beads."

Visualize this intention as a wave moving through you and see how far you can follow it. When you feel that you have tracked your intention as far as you can, open your eyes and see if you notice a shift within yourself. Has stating your intention helped you enter into the creative process with more ease? Has following your intention led you toward your sacred center?

Try stating the intention to use beading to help you find your sacred center, and see what happens. Intention is a very powerful tool that *you* can use to awaken consciousness and direct your art in a more creative, spiritual direction.

10. Wildness

As the final tool of creative expression, wildness is the spark that ignites our creativity. As Clarissa Pinkola Estés wrote in *Women Who Run with the Wolves,* wildness (also known as the Wild Woman archetype) is the force behind our innate instinctual nature. All creative people need to have a little wildness inside them. The Wild Woman is our creative fire and what drives us to make art; we cannot live without her. Our creative spontaneity and imagination depend on wildness, but we do need to kindle her and tend to her. We also need to acknowledge her presence. As the patroness of all creative people, she waits to be beckoned forward.

You can do this simply by using your imagination to greet and embrace her as you welcome her into your beading space. Invite her to come and dance with you while you bead; throw back your head and howl with her to really get her creative energy moving through you. Reconnecting with your wildness can set you free to be your innate creative self. Your beading will never be the same again!

◉◉◉

Each one of these ten tools can help you feel more connected to the Creative Spirit that lives within you. Think of them as friends and mentors in your creative process. They are always available to you, always supportive of you. Acknowledge them whenever you can. Love, in particular, only multiplies and grows stronger when you are open to its transformative, healing energies. In your spiritual journey, love will always be the foundation upon which you can build and sustain your creative life. Every one of the tools of creative expression is within you, waiting to be picked up and used to support your creativity. It is up to you to make the choice to utilize them; they need to be nurtured, just like a friendship.

Wearing the Tool Belt of Creative Expression can remind you that each tool is always available right at your fingertips.

Cripplers of Creative Expression

Just as there are tools that support our creative expression, there are also feelings that cripple our creativity and hold it hostage. Because they are common within each of us, it is important to mention them. Sometimes just becoming aware of when they get activated can help release their grip and free us from their debilitating or paralyzing constraints.

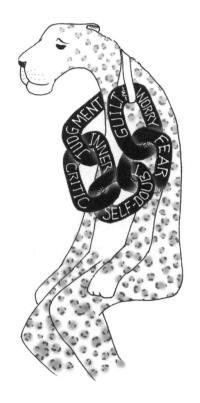

1. Guilt and Worry

Guilt and worry are opposite ends of the same spectrum. Guilt is built around being immobilized as a result of past behavior, and worry immobilizes us in the present about something that might or might not happen in the future (and that we most likely have no control over). Both guilt and worry prevent us from being fully in the *now,* and both are totally useless, debilitating behaviors.

No amount of guilt can change what happened in the past. No amount of worry can change what will happen in the future. We are wasting our precious present-moment energy if we obsess about something we have done or said in the past, or did not do or say. The same can be said of worrying about some future event.

Beading, because it is a present-moment activity, can be helpful in overcoming feelings of guilt or worry. If you find yourself caught up in guilt or worry, get out your beads and start working on a project, *any* project. Just the act of beading will bring you into the present and help you refocus, so you can benefit from the positive effects of the creative stimulation.

2. Fear

Another major crippler of creative expression is fear. Fear of the unknown or fear of failure can cause resistance to new experiences, rigidity, prejudice, or perfectionism. Each of these behaviors can sabotage our creativity and prevent us from taking that "road less traveled." Fear can also cause us to see change as a threat. Yet life is predicated on change. To live is to change. Allowing ourselves to be flexible and open to the changes in our lives can help us grow through the changes rather than be paralyzed by them.

In both a symbolic and literal way, beadwork can help you to overcome your fear of the unknown and to embrace change. Free-form beading, for example, is a wonderful exercise in being able to change direction within a piece, as well as being able to head off into unknown territory. There is no such thing as a "mistake." If you do not like something, take it out or go back over it enough times that you cannot see it anymore.

I once decided to make a free-form necklace using just black and pink beads, something I had never tried before. When it was almost completed, I studied it closely and realized that the black beads were too dominant in the overall color composition of the necklace. So I beaded back over the black beads with more pink ones to soften the impact of the black, and the result was a better color balance. The fear of experimenting could have prevented me from even starting the project, but trust in the creative process helped push me through any fears I had about "failing."

3. Self-Doubt

There is healthy self-doubt, and there is unhealthy self-doubt. Unhealthy self-doubt can stop us dead in our tracks and make it impossible to move forward. It can prevent us from being able to make choices because we doubt we will make the "right" choice.

Beading, like life, is all about making choices: choices in what beads to use, in what sizes, in what colors, even in what project to start or finish. Everything in beading involves having to make decisions. The next time you are beading, take a few minutes to assess your doubt level. Unhealthy self-doubt can cause you to continually second guess yourself. It can prevent you from enjoying your beading time, as well as dampen any spark of creativity that might be present.

Healthy self-doubt, on the other hand, can act as a filter that you place over a decision you need to make. It might stop you long enough to study what you are working on when you come to a crossroads and are ready to shift direction or make a color change, or when you are just not sure where you are going on your piece and need to look at it for awhile before you are ready to continue. Healthy self-doubt can give you enough time to study the choice you need to make more closely, weighing your options before making your decision. When you are ready, you can break through the filter of healthy doubt and act from a place of conviction and renewed self-confidence. This form of self-doubt can be life affirming rather than crippling. Healthy self-doubt can be an ally in your creative endeavor while unhealthy self-doubt can sabotage it.

4. Inner Critic

Our Inner Critic is the voice in our head that is constantly criticizing us: "Who do you think you are, anyway? You're too fat, too thin, too tall, too short, too stupid, too smart for your own good. You can't draw or paint or bead. You aren't creative." Our Inner Critic sabotages and tries to short-circuit our attempts to be creative, so we need to pay close attention when she shows up—because she always will!

When you are beading, the voice of your Inner Critic can be so loud, it can prevent you from being creative in your work. A first step in being able to release your Inner Critic's hold on you is to recognize when she has shown up, and listen to what she has to say. Then a dialog can take place between the right hemisphere of your brain (where your creativity dwells) and the left hemisphere (where your Inner Critic sits on her throne).

Bead artist/teacher Nancy Eha, in her book *Off the Beadin' Path,* gives an excellent method for dealing with your Inner Critic. Briefly, she suggests making a list of the negative messages that you receive from your "abusive authoritarian voice." After making the list, she suggests you come up with positive affirmations that counteract the negative messages. If you write down every negative message you hear in your head, you can shift the energy by saying your positive affirmation as a response. It will take time for this method to be effective, but you need to remember that it took time for your Inner Critic to grow so powerful, and it will take time to silence her. Humor helps!

5. Judgment

There is another archetypal essence that can be so crippling to creativity that it stops its flow: the Judge who pronounces judgment on our creative life. Similar to our Inner Critic, the Judge sits in our dominant left brain and doles out judgment about everything we do in life. Usually this judgment concerns itself with behavior that is deemed right/wrong, good/bad, or black/white.

When you bead, you need to banish the Judge whenever she shows up and tries to pass judgment on what you are making. You can do this by first becoming aware of whenever your Judge is sitting in her seat of judgment and issuing statements to you such as, "This isn't good enough … that is so bad … you'll never make anything beautiful … you should stop trying to be creative because whatever you make will never be good enough…." As soon as you become aware of these destructive comments, you can start to shift them. As with your Inner Critic, positive affirmations are an effective tool to counteract the judgmental ones.

Recently, "her Honor" issued a judgment statement to me: "Why bother entering a piece of your beadwork in that competition? Other people's work has gotten so intricate and sophisticated that yours won't be half as good." My positive affirmation for that criticism was, "The work I make is empowered with Divine Spirit, from which it derives its value and meaning."

When you are beading, it is important not to compare yourself with anyone else or to compare the creative work you make with anyone else's. If you do, you can fall into the trap of judgment that is almost impossible to get out of and that certainly inhibits creativity. "Thou shalt not compare!" is a good commandment to keep in mind to help prevent this from happening in your beadwork.

The Spiral of Growth

I like to visualize the spiral as a symbol that represents the force of the Creative Spirit. For me, it is a symbol of the Creative Spirit as an energetic power that is active and dynamic. The spiral is a universal symbol found in cultures worldwide, dating back to Paleolithic times. It has many meanings and often has multiple levels within a meaning. For instance, the spiral can represent the revolving heavens, the course of the sun, the cyclical seasons, and the rotation of the earth. As the whirl of the air in thunder, tornadoes, and the movement of the oceans, it denotes fertility and the dynamic aspects of life.

Journalist Geoff Ward, in his book *Spirals: The Pattern of Existence,* refers to the spiral as the symbolic pattern of human spiritual growth. It can symbolize a vortex and the great creative force from which all life emanates. As a spherical vortex, spiraling through its own center, it combines both inward and outward directions of movement, symbolizing the process of our growth and evolution.

The two projects in this chapter, a Dutch Spiral Necklace and a Spiral Vessel, are based on spiral symbols. For the first project, I have included an exercise in drawing spirals as a way of connecting you to the rhythmic patterns that are contained within the flow of the movement of spirals.

For the second project, I offer a meditation on the internal spiral of your living cell nuclei known as deoxyribonucleic acid (DNA). This beautiful double helix is a spiral that contains all of your essential genetic material that makes you *you*!

EXERCISE
Drawing Spirals

Before you begin Project 11, I suggest you take a few minutes to do the following exercise. It will help you find the rhythm of this spiraling stitch.

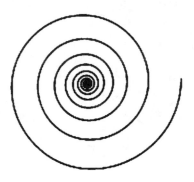

Spiral sketch.

This is an exercise in drawing spirals. For inspiration, think of Stone Age drawings in caves and on rock formations. Think of the whorls of a Celtic cross or the facial tattoos of a Maori chief from New Zealand. Spirals are found in Islamic architecture, Navajo sand paintings, the tentacles of an octopus, and our inner ear. Our DNA molecule is a spiral; water going down a drain is a spiral. You may use the sketch of the spiral to the left as an example to get you started doing this exercise, though you are welcome to draw any form of a spiral that inspires you.

1. Take a blank sheet of paper and pencil and begin to draw a spiral design. If you have a specific type of spiral in mind, work in that direction. Otherwise, simply let the spiral take shape as it flows onto your paper.

2. As you are drawing, notice how you are feeling. You are working with a universal symbol that is full of meaning on many levels. How are you reacting to it?

3. Give yourself permission to play as you draw several different spirals.

4. Feel your hand and your body connect to the rhythm of the spiraling movement as you are drawing. Try drawing the spiral moving in both directions, inward and outward, and observe how this motion affects you internally, if at all. Is the motion pulling you internally as it gets smaller and smaller? Is it pushing your energy externally as it grows bigger and bigger?

5. Once you can feel the rhythmic motion of drawing spirals, the rhythmic motion of beading in a spiraling format will come more easily. Every beading stitch has its own rhythm, and once you learn the rhythm of a particular stitch, it becomes imprinted in your hands and your brain, making it much easier to do.

6. When you are ready, you may end the drawing exercise and begin beading your Dutch Spiral Necklace.

Dutch Spiral Necklace

Dutch Spiral Necklaces,
Wendy Ellsworth, 2007.
(For a color photograph of this project, with examples of possible color combinations, see color plate 7a.)

This is a fun project using a spiraling form of the gourd (peyote) stitch to create a lovely necklace. There are many variations on this Dutch spiral. My version includes four different sizes of seed beads, so there is plenty of room for color variations. Each beading stitch continues the spiraling motion around and around as each row builds upon the beads already added. You can continue making rows until the necklace is the length you want it to be. As you are beading, notice how the rhythm of making a continual spiral affects you. Perhaps you will find it soothing and meditative.

MATERIALS

- Seed beads in four sizes and colors:
    Color 1: size 6, 10 grams (for spiral beads)
    Color 2: size 8, 10 grams (for spiral beads)
    Color 3: size 11, 10 grams (for spiral beads)
    Color 4: size 15, 10 grams (for chain beads)

- Silamide thread size A or Nymo size B
- Sharps short beading needles, size 12
- Button with a shank or a clasp of your choice
- Scissors
- Beading mat
- Ott light or desk lamp

PROJECT PREPARATION

- Pull off approximately 9 feet of thread and prestretch it by pulling it out between your hands, working your way along its entire length.
- Thread your needle and bring it to the middle of the thread.
- Work with your thread doubled. Do not knot the thread.

Row 1

(see figure 6.1)

- Pick up one size-6, one size-8, one size-11, and four size-15 seed beads.
- Run them down to within 12 inches of the ends of your thread. (You will use the ends or "tails" of your thread to finish the necklace, so do not cut them off.)
- Pass the thread back through all the beads a second time, pulling them into a circle, with the thread coming out of the size-6 bead to be in place to begin row 2.

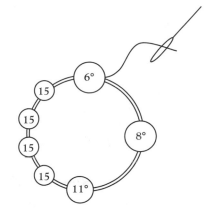

6.1. Dutch Spiral Necklace, row 1.

Row 2

(see figure 6.2)

- Pick up one size-8 bead and stitch into the size-8 bead in row 1.
- Pick up one size-11 bead and stitch into the size-11 bead in row 1.
- Pick up five size-15 beads and one size-6 bead and stitch into the size-6 bead in row 1.
- Notice that whatever bead you pick up will be the same size bead you stitch into next.
- *Note:* Figure 6.2 shows row 2 completed and the first size-8 bead for row 3 on the thread ready to be stitched into the size-8 from row 2.

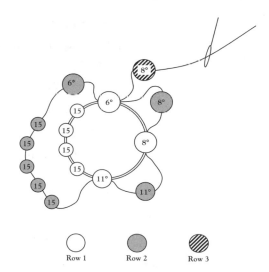

6.2. Dutch Spiral Necklace, row 2.

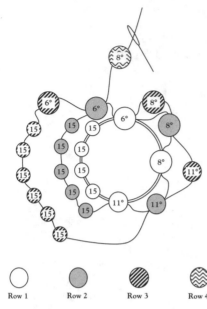

6.3. Dutch Spiral Necklace, row 3.

Row 3

(see figure 6.3)

- Repeat the instructions for row 2, increasing the number of size-15 beads to six.

You will notice that the bead you pick up needs to match the bead you are about to stitch into from row 2. So, a size-8 bead will be stitched into the size-8 from row 2, a size-11 bead will be stitched into the size-11 from row 2, and the size-15 beads together with the size-6 bead will be stitched into the size-6 from row 2. This is what makes the necklace spiral as each row feeds directly into the next one without a step-up to demarcate the end of a row and the beginning of the next one. Like all forms of the gourd stitch, each new row builds off the beads of the previous row.

Rows 4 and 5

- Increase the number of size-15 beads by one in rows 4 and 5. You will end up with eight size-15 beads in row 5.

Rows 6 and up

- Repeat the instructions for row 2 (using a total of eight size-15 beads for each spiral row) until the necklace is the length you desire.

You may keep increasing the number of size-15 beads if you want to. That will change the look of the overall necklace. The beads will naturally spiral, row after row, in a fun rhythm that works up quickly.

Adding Thread

When adding a new thread, I suggest using the method that I find most useful. The principle stays the same no matter what stitch you are working in.

- You need to stop working with the old thread and lay the project aside for the moment.
- Pull off approximately 9 feet of new thread and prestretch it by pulling it out between your hands, working your way along its entire length.
- Thread a new needle and it bring to the middle of the thread. Work with your thread doubled. Do not knot the thread.
- Weave this new thread into your project so that it ends up coming out of the same bead as the old thread, putting one or two slip knots around several threads along the way to secure it.
- Tie the new thread to the old thread with a square knot.
- Take the old thread and weave it through a few beads. You can put a slip knot around a thread to secure it. Cut it off to end it.
- Cut off the tail of the new thread and continue beading.

To End Necklace

- Decrease the number of size-15 beads by one in each row until you have a total of four size-15 beads, as you had in row 1. (If you stayed with eight size-15 beads each spiral, it will take a total of four rows to complete the decrease.)

FINISHING

- Add a button with a shank or whatever clasp you have chosen for it onto the end of your necklace. There is no one way to do this. Be creative and experiment with it!
- End the thread.
- At the opposite end of the necklace, thread a needle onto the two threads of the original tail (they should both be able to fit through the eye of your needle together) and make a loop that will fit over the button (or add the other side of the clasp). You may want to stitch back through the loop a second time to make it stronger.
- End the thread.

◎◎◎

Before you begin Project 12, I recommend the following guided meditation that focuses on the symbol of the spiral and, in particular, the double spiral helix that forms your DNA. Your DNA represents the essence of your genetic material, the internal core of who you are. The Spiral Vessel project represents an external form of your spiral journey through life. While the Spiral Vessels shown are closed forms, you may find that your vessel needs to be left open at the top, indicating the continuation of your journey that is yet to come.

Meditation
Spirals

1. Begin your meditation by creating a space and time where you will not be disturbed.
2. Sit quietly and take three deep breaths, releasing tension on your exhalations from those places where you tend to hold it in your body.
3. Gently close your eyes.
4. Keep focused on your breathing and let any chatter from your "monkey mind" softly fade away.
5. Visualize a spiral in your mind's eye. It can be a sea shell, the horns of a bighorn sheep, a coiled up snake, or a fern unfolding. Whatever spiral image you picture, examine the spiral closely in your mind's eye, following its pattern from one end to the other.
6. Visualize another example of a natural spiral and follow its pattern both inward and outward.
7. Now visualize the double helix spiral of your chain of DNA. Acknowledge its presence inside of you. It is what makes you *you*! Can you sense its spiraling motion?

8. Imagine your DNA in the shape of a coiling ladder with rungs that link the two interweaving strands of DNA. These rungs are like steps on a spiral staircase that has a total of about three billion rungs on it! Think of it as a huge library full of information about you. Can you read some of what is written there? The hidden secret of life is found within the spiral code of your DNA. Every organism on earth shares this code with you. This is how we are all interconnected with one another.

9. Feel the oneness of this DNA code that connects us to all that exists on this beautiful planet. Breathe in oneness, breathe out oneness. Continue this for awhile.

10. Shift your awareness now to your Crown chakra. Visualize it as a spinning vortex that is spiraling counterclockwise above your head as you open it.

11. Imagine a beam of shimmering light streaming and spiraling down through your Crown chakra into your body. Let yourself be filled up with this radiant light. Look carefully at the filaments of light as they flow through you; they are bringing information for you. What do they have to tell you? Can you open to receive it?

12. Gently open your eyes and look around the room. You may want to write down what you experienced or learned so you will remember it later. You may also wish to express gratitude for any guidance you have received during the meditation.

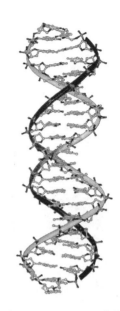

A representation of the DNA double helix.

Spiral Vessel

Spiral Vessels,
Wendy Ellsworth, 2001.
(For a color photograph of this project, see color plate 7b.)

This is a free-form vessel that begins by working in flat circular gourd stitch that starts from the center of the bottom of the vessel. In order to make the walls rise, you stop increasing the number of beads in the rows, tighten the tension, and direct the beads upward with your fingers. Once the walls are going upward, you will automatically be working in tubular gourd stitch. It becomes "free-form" when you play around with increasing and decreasing to make it change its shape.

MATERIALS

- Seed beads, size 6, in nine colors, approximately 5 grams each for six of the colors, and approximately 36 grams each for three of them (see Project Preparation)
- Cube beads, 4 millimeters, in three colors, approximately 5 grams each
- Nymo thread, size D or F
- Sharps short beading needles, size 10
- Scissors
- Beading mat
- Ott light or desk lamp

PROJECT PREPARATION

Note: The directions for this project involve numbering each one of the colors you use to make the vessel. The total number of colors is twelve. In the directions, I use a capital C to indicate each color. For example, color 1 is indicated as C1.

- Arrange your beads in two rows with six piles of beads in each row, following the key of bead types in figure 6.4.

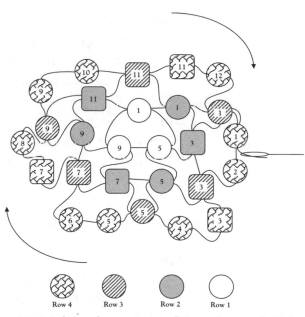

6.4. Numbering system for bead colors.

- Place the size-6 beads, for which you have 5 grams of each color, in piles 1, 4, 5, 8, 9, 12. (*Note:* The beads in piles 1, 5, and 9 will tend to stay in a single line when you make the project.)
- Place the size-6 beads, for which you have 36 grams of each color, in piles 2, 6, 10. These will be the dominant color bands.
- Place the cube beads in piles 3, 7, and 11.
- Number each pile so you do not lose track.
- Pull off approximately 5 yards of thread. Prestretch the thread and add your needle. Work the thread doubled. Do not knot tails.

Row 1

- Pick up one bead each from piles 1, 5, and 9. (I will refer to them as C1, C5, and C9.)
- Slide them down to approximately 4 inches from the ends of the thread and pass back through (PBT) all three beads again in the same direction, exiting from C1. They will form a triangle.

Row 2

Working in flat circular gourd stitch, increase as follows:

- Pick up one bead from C1 and C3. Stitch into the next bead (bead 5 in figure 6.5).
- Pick up one bead from C5 and C7. Stitch into the next bead (bead 9 in figure 6.5).

6.5. Spiral Vessel, rows 1–4, in flat circular gourd stitch.

- Pick up one bead from C9 and C11. Stitch into the next bead (bead 1 from row 1 in figure 6.5)
- Step-up to be in position to begin row 3 by also stitching through the first bead of the row just completed (bead 1 from row 2) This step-up will be repeated for each new row and will always be in C1!

Row 3

- Pick up one bead after each bead in row 2. (Match the bead you pick up to the bead your thread is exiting.) This is called a "radical" increase. (See figure 6.5.)
- The sequence will be: C1, C3, C5, C7, C9, C11.
- Step-up to be in position to begin the next row.

Row 4

- Pick up two beads after each bead in row 3 as follows: C1 and C2, C3 and C4, C5 and C6, C7 and C8, C9 and C10, C11 and C12.
- Step-up. (This is as far as figure 6.5 goes.)

Rows 5 and 6

- Pick up a bead after each bead in the previous row. Match the bead you pick up to the bead your thread is exiting.
- Step-up after each row.

Row 7

- Pick up a bead after each bead in the previous row as follows (note the increases): one C1, two C2s, one C3, one C4, one C5, two C6s, one C7, one C8, one C9, two C10s, one C11, one C12.
- Step-up.

Row 8

- Pick up a bead after each bead in the previous row, matching the bead you pick up to the bead your thread is exiting.

- When you come to the row 7 increases in C2, C6, and C10, place a bead between the two beads (a radical increase).
- Step-up.

Row 9

- Pick up a bead after each bead in the previous row as follows (note the increases): one C1, two C2s, two C2s, one C3, one C4, one C5, two C6s, two C6s, one C7, one C8, one C9, two C10s, two C10s, one C11, one C12.
- Step-up.

Row 10

- Pick up a bead after each bead in the previous row (including increases) as in row 8.
- Step-up.

Row 11

- Pick up a bead after each bead in the previous row as in row 10.
- Step-up.

Row 12

- Pick up a bead after each bead in the previous row as in row 11.
- If your beads show a wide gap or you want to expand the circumference, make a two-bead increase when you reach the second stitch of C2, C6, and C10.
- Step-up.

Row 13

- Pick up a bead after each bead in row 12.
- If you increased in row 12, place a bead between the two, as in row 8.
- Step-up.

Rows 14 and 15

- Pick up a bead after each bead in the previous row.
- Tighten the tension and pull the beads upward to begin shaping the vessel walls; or, to increase the circumference, make two-bead increases as in row 12.
- As always, make a step-up to end each row to be in position to begin the next row.

Rows 16 to end

The Spiral Vessels shown in color plate 7b have different numbers of rows since one is larger than the other. The increases and decreases you make in these rows determine the vessel's finished profile. The walls curve outward when you increase. You control the extent of the bulging by the frequency and placement of additional beads. Remember to work a radical increase, as in row 3, when you stitch into the next row.

FINISHING

To bring the walls inward, decrease over two or four rows as follows, keeping the tension very tight (*Note:* See chapter 3, Project 5, figures 3.10 and 3.11, for decreasing in gourd stitch):

- First decrease row: Stitch into the next bead in sequence without adding a bead.
- Second and third decrease rows: When you come to the decrease, place one or two beads in the gap.
- If you added one bead, the decrease is complete. If you added two beads, treat them as one when you stitch the third row.
- Fourth decrease row: In the fourth row, put only a single bead where you placed the two to complete the decrease.

Vessel Design

The design of your Spiral Vessel will be unique. As the walls go up, you can shape them by adding increases or by making decreases. You can bring the form in and then let it bulge out again into a ruffle. You may want to make a vessel that is open at the top. Another possibility is to close up the form completely, as in my *Spiral Vessels* pictured in color plate 7b. It is your journey up the spiral that matters most, and where it takes you is your destination alone. Like life, you may be surprised by its twists and turns; even when the project is completed, the spiral journey of your life will continue on. Travel it gently.

Bead Your Bliss

Sing Your Song

*Sing your own song of happiness in any way that
you choose, oblivious to how it is supposed to be.*

—Wayne Dyer

Song of Joy and Passion

Each of us is unique. We have our own identity, our own joys and
sorrows, our own journey through life. Each of us also has an
energy frequency or pulse that is ours alone. If you think about
energy frequency as a vibration, which is really a pattern of sound
waves, it follows that our unique sound could be called our "voice"
or our "Song." Another way to say this is that our Song is the sound
of our spirit's unique vibrations.

According to spiritual healer Kay Cordell Whitaker, author of
Sacred Link, our Song provides us with the dream and the power to
persist through the challenges of the journeys of spiritual growth.
It is the tool that connects us with the joy and passion of life that is
our unique identity. Each of us has the opportunity to find our
Song, to learn to sing it with our own voice.

Singing our Song brings us into contact with bliss, that state of grace known as *sat chit ananda,* a Sanskrit term where *sat* translates into "being," *chit* translates into "consciousness," and *ananda* translates into "bliss" or "rapture."

When mythologist Joseph Campbell admonished us to "follow your bliss," he was, in essence, saying that the mission of life is to live the potentiality we are born with. He felt that we continually have experiences that our intuition senses as blissful, and we need to grab hold of them and follow where they lead us. But in order to do this, we need to recognize our own depth and direction and not let anyone pull us off track. When we find our unique Song and sing it with passion, many of life's possibilities open up doors where we had no idea they would occur. Going through these portals leads us to our destiny, which is a validation of our life choices and actions we have taken.

When I have followed my Song, it has led me to places and people I never could have anticipated. Who knows what trajectory my life would have taken if I had chosen the "safe" path. Had I followed my parents' way, for example, I would never have married my first husband or become a bead artist. Instead, I followed Campbell's advice to "follow my bliss," even though I had never heard of Campbell at the time. I just knew at the depth of my being that I had to shift course and change the direction I had been headed; eventually this decision led me to discover the Song of my soul's joy through the art of beading.

Campbell taught that we cannot have creativity unless we leave behind those things in our life that are fixed, immobile, and bounded by rules and listen to our own intuition. Only then can we create from our place of bliss. I have experienced this place through beadwork. Through beading, I feel truly alive and present in the now. It contributes to my passion for living. Over the many years I have been beading, I have been able to develop a body of work that is uniquely my expression of the Creative Spirit, my unique voice within the field of beadwork artistry. My Song is perhaps most recognizable in my SeaForm series of beaded three-dimensional sculptures.

In the moment of creative expression, you can feel this passion for living that contributes to being able to find and sing your Song. Finding your bliss through beading is not only enjoyable and fun, it can also potentially bring you to the transformative state of *sat chit ananda*. When you experience the spiritual joy of singing your Song through beadwork, you will have discovered the sacred center within.

Tanjung Samba SeaForm, Wendy Ellsworth, 6 x 7 x 6 inches, glass seed beads, daggers, thread, etched blown-glass base, 2008.

Beads of Our Song

There are many "beads" or qualities that make up the expression of our Song, and I have identified ten in particular. Each one is an aspect of our authentic voice, that beautiful vibration or sound that is our unique identity. I believe that these ten beads of our Song are innate within each of us. Through them, you can discover your real voice and express your original Song. I have made a beaded bead for each one of these ten qualities; collectively, I refer to them as "Song Beads."

1. Passion

Passion is a life force that stimulates, excites, and exalts us with its power. It is an absolutely necessary and primary stimulant for being creative. We cannot sing our Song without it. Passion flows through us into expression, and we can use passion to motivate us to birth new ideas into physical form. Passion is almost boundless in its ability to charge us up emotionally, physically, psychologically, and spiritually. Our passions can elevate us into states of ecstasy, into *sat chit ananda,* where we can become excessively exuberant. Who can resist that form of bliss and joy?

Each of us is passionate about many things. Beaders whom I know certainly tend to be passionate about beads and the act of beading itself. I am convinced this is what has led to a renaissance

Song Bead 1.

of interest in beading over recent years. Many people are now beading their bliss because they have become passionate about beads. More and more people are discovering their passion for beading and using it as their form of creative expression.

If you are a beader but do not feel passion for your beaded creations, it might be helpful to ask yourself some questions: What *does* bring me passion? Where do I feel passion in my life? What is holding me back from feeling passionate about what I create? What can I change to allow passion back into my life and into my beading?

Asking yourself these kinds of questions will begin to open the doors to what is blocking you from your passion. It is a vital life force that is behind every creative act you participate in, and it is the foundation bead of your Song.

2. Persistence

Persistence accompanies passion. Without persistence, we might not be able to push through the obstacles that life often seems to place in our way. Persistence means having the guts and fortitude to stay with our Song no matter what happens. If we have persistence, we can be tested and retested and still maintain our purpose and intention. When the road leads us places we never expected to go, persistence can help us continue the journey when the going gets rough.

Song Bead 2.

As we are beading, persistence can help us find the inner strength to keep singing our Song when we are faced with doubt and criticism. I think of the craft artists I know who have persisted for years in trying to get into the Philadelphia Museum of Art Craft Show and eventually made it. My own beadwork was finally accepted into this show in 1996. Because there was no official category for "beads or beadwork," I had to choose another category in which to enter my work. I chose the glass medium because I worked with glass beads and placed my SeaForms on hand-blown glass bases. When the work was accepted in the glass category, I was happily surprised and pleased. My persistence had paid off!

How do you relate to persistence? When you are working on a piece of beadwork, do you find yourself giving up easily? When you run into difficulties, do you get frustrated and stop working on how to figure out the problem? If so, try remembering the gift of persistence; tell yourself that this is just a momentary block or challenge, and use persistence to push through it. Persistence is a valuable bead to add to your Song.

3. Commitment

Once we have found our authentic, creative voice, we need to decide what our commitment is to singing our Song. For some, beading will be a wonderful hobby. Others may find themselves wanting to make beading more of a priority. When I decided that I was ready to grow my bead art, I made a commitment to go into my bead studio every day. Metaphorically, I put some of my friendships and old commitments up on a shelf, knowing that someday I would take them down again. My passion and commitment to singing my Song with beads was stronger than any fears I had about letting some things go, and I chose to make this sacrifice in order to focus on my beadwork. It was a commitment I made from a place of loving myself enough to give myself permission to go into my studio and make art.

What kind of a commitment do you want to make to grow your bead art? Is commitment an important part of you singing your Song? What level of priority do you want to give it? What might that mean in terms of the time and space you allot to beading? What do you need to say to friends and family to be clear about what you need to honor your commitment? Your responses

Song Bead 3.

to these questions will show you what level of priority commitment has in singing your Song through the art of beadwork.

4. Freedom

Another bead of our Song is freedom. When we are singing our Song, it brings a newfound freedom of expression and sets our Spirit free. With this freedom comes a level of feeling truly alive that is transformative. Freedom brings with it tremendous power. As with passion and commitment, it is an energetic force that moves through us, and once we connect with it, chances are we will not ever let go of it. Freedom carries within it a resilience that we can depend on as we sing the Song of our authentic, creative self.

Song Bead 4.

I think of the Samburu and Maasai women in Kenya with whom I have worked. In these two tribes women are, for all intents and purposes, "owned" by their husbands, who have paid a bride price for them and do not want them to know that they have any rights to personal freedom. My goal is to teach these women new beading techniques and product designs aimed specifically at export in order for them to achieve a new level of personal freedom in their lives. As they learn to sing their Song through their beadwork, their commitment, persistence, and passion are incredibly strong and support them in their journey to personal freedom. When they sing their Songs in unison, they have the strength and power to overcome the many obstacles that continue to be placed in their way.

Where does freedom fit into your life and the choices you make? Do you take risks in your creative work? What happens when you do? What happens when you don't? If your fears are holding you back, can you see what is behind your fear of taking a risk? What can you do to start claiming freedom for yourself? If you want to sing your Song, you will need this bead of personal freedom!

5. Wholeness

When we are able to sing our Song, we are living from a place of wholeness. And as we achieve wholeness internally, we will also be able to feel a part of the greater wholeness. We will be interconnected to the great web of life, to Gaia, our beautiful planet Earth. And when we feel part of the greater whole, we have more access to the beauty and wonder that is around us and will be better able to recreate it through our art.

Attaining wholeness does not mean that there is no more room to grow and change. Wholeness is not a static state of being; rather, it is a state of complete aliveness that is open to growth and change—two essential keys to life. Being flexible is another key to wholeness. As we sing our Song from a place of wholeness, we will know what it feels like to have the flexibility of a tall tree blowing in a strong wind. Deeply rooted and grounded in our wholeness, we will have the flexibility to gracefully bend with whatever life blows our way.

Song Bead 5.

I think of Karen Paust, who is a seed bead artist who has found her own voice within the field of beadwork. What a beautiful Song she sings! She works with only the tiniest seed beads (sizes 22 and 24), creating botanically accurate flowers, plants, vegetables, insects, moths, and butterflies, turning them into necklaces that are glorious in their intricate detail. In 1989, while she was living in California, her home and studio were completely destroyed by a fast-moving forest fire, and she lost everything: all of her possessions and all of her precious beads. A plea went out among the beading community with the request to send her a new stash of beads so she could get back to work again. And beaders responded by overwhelming her with gifts of even more beads than she had had to begin with. Remaining flexible helped her deal with the changes life had so suddenly blown her way, and she emerged reenergized and transformed by the love so

Polyphemus Moth, Karen Paust, 3 x 6 inches, glass beads, thread, wire, wood, sterling silver, 1998. (Photograph by T. E. Crowley.)

many strangers had shown her. She continued to sing her Song and bead her bliss from a place of wholeness that is inspirational.

What do you need in order to feel whole? How can the art of beading help you achieve this? Can you use your beadwork to feel connected to all the other people in the world who are beading? Together we make up a whole that is greater than the sum of its parts: we form the "field" of beadwork and each of us is an integral member! Each of us has our own unique Song to share within the wholeness of our beading field.

6. Vision

To be able to bead with our authentic Song, we need personal vision. Vision allows us to explore the possibilities of what direction our beadwork might take. Without vision, our beadwork will tend to be derivative, a copy of someone else's vision. Our vision is a part of our spiritual essence that we need to tap into before we can take any creative action. We need to look within—at our dreams, our desires, our intentions, and our imagination. From these places, we spark our personal vision, opening up possibilities that we can explore with our thoughts and eventually with our needles, thread, and beads. Something external may also trigger our personal vision, but it still takes shape as an internal force, driven by our curiosity and the passion to create.

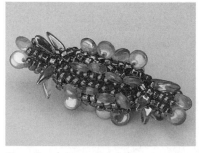

Song Bead 6.

In 2007 I was invited to submit examples of my bead art for a book titled *Masters: Beadweaving.* It is a treasure trove of photos that show how thirty-six bead artists are singing their Songs through the personal vision they bring to their beadwork. Many more bead artists are contributing their unique vision to the field of beading, too. In particular, artists who are now coming out of universities with BFAs and MFAs are discovering the potential for working with beads and are adding their original visions to the medium, as well.

As a beader, what is your vision for what you want to create with your beads? Are you like some of my students, who hope they live long enough to make all the things they envision? There is an infinite source of possibilities when it comes to what to make with your beads. If you need a few ideas to stimulate your vision, meditating or getting together with other beaders might be helpful. Sometimes a bead society will have a bead challenge that will invigorate your vision. Once you get started, the ideas will keep flowing. You just have to turn on the spigot of your wonderful, creative imagination!

7. *Integrity*

Integrity is a vital element of the expression of our personal Song. Integrity implies a level of personal honesty that begins with our core self and from there radiates out into every aspect of our creative life. Personal integrity shines from the inside out and will be reflected in the work we make.

Integrity also denotes a sincere level of truthfulness that finds full expression in our creative actions. If we do not have personal integrity, our beadwork will also lack this vital elemental force. If someone copies another person's beadwork and presents it as her own, she is being dishonest and untruthful, both of which reflect a lack of integrity. I see this in the beading field, particularly within the realm of teaching classes and submitting articles for publication. People copy other people's work, make a slight change, and submit it as curriculum for a class or for publication in the beading magazines. Beaders need to think carefully about where they get their ideas and give credit where credit is due, both to their teachers and to

Song Bead 7.

the other influences on their work. Personal integrity is basic to our creative truth.

Where do you rate yourself on the scale of personal integrity? It is easy to think we have "invented" something new and then discover that others have already used the same idea. If this is your experience, take what I call the "laugh" test. If you see someone else's beading that is close to yours, can you laugh about it and enjoy a connection to that person? If there is real integrity on the part of both beaders, there will be a sense of humor involved that will reveal that each of you was merely beading your own bliss and managed to come up with similar concepts. Neither copied the other person's work. This happens all the time in every craft/art medium. Can you laugh about it? Integrity with humor is always honest.

8. *Authenticity*

Our Song is a direct manifestation of our true self, and the expression of our authentic self in our bead Song can have many forms. Bead artists are expressing their authentic voice in many remarkable ways. They are using their bead Song to express their anger, their

Song Bead 8.

pain, their joy, their happiness, their hurt, their sadness, their grief, their curiosity, their bliss; the list goes on and on.

JoAnn Baumann is a bead artist whose work reflects her sincere approach to life. Her beadwork is a reflection of her personal journey and continual search to find and redefine herself. She is in search of her authentic self, and her bead art is a reflection of her curiosity about her life's many experiences. Her piece *Not This One* relates directly to her experience with breast cancer, a disease that affects so many women today.

JoAnn handles some of her musings on life with delicious humor and brilliant color, leading the viewer to try to imagine what was going through her head when she came up with her ideas. She is a master of the bead-weaving medium, and authenticity is a crucial bead in her Song.

What is your bead Song? How are you using beads to express your authenticity? How are you processing your feelings through your beadwork? Can you see how this process is a doorway leading to your authentic self? When you express your authentic self through your beadwork, you will be on the road to "beading your bliss" and singing your own Song of joy and passion.

Not This One, JoAnn Baumann, 12 x 13 x 2 inches, seed beads, thread, bra, hand-marbled silk, 2004. (Photograph by Larry Sanders.)

9. Intuition

Intuition is a feeling sense that comes from deep within us, usually from our gut. Actually, there are more neural pathways in our gut than in our brain, so it is fitting that we sometimes refer to our intuition as our gut instinct.

For creative work, intuition plays an active role in helping us intuit our way into and through a project. Intuition is like a flashlight: it can help guide us with its light through the vast unfamiliar territory that we find ourselves in when we start off on a new journey of creative expression. If we can learn to rely on our intuition to show us the way, we will have more trust in the unknown aspects of the creative process and, hopefully, be less fearful of getting started.

Bead artist Gail Gorlitzz explains that when she starts a project, she begins with an issue she wants to work through in the making of the piece. It could be a color, spatial, or subject challenge, although often all three are involved. The tiny increments of the beading and the slow, repetitive process facilitate her practice of allowing the conscious mind to be overtaken by the intuitive mind. This produces the organic nature of her work. As the project progresses, if something unanticipated

Song Bead 9.

does not emerge to fully engage her attention, she either changes the piece or abandons it. She has no preconception of what the piece will look like when it is finished, so each one is a journey into the unknown, with intuition as her guiding mentor.

Eye Sea, Gail Gorlitzz, 26 x 18 x 8 inches, glass, cord, metal, plastic, 2005. (Photograph by Jay Mallin.)

Take a moment to reflect on your own intuition. See if you can sense where it is located in your body. Perhaps it is just a deep "knowing" that does not have an exact location, but you know it is in there somewhere. Do you trust your intuition when it speaks to you? How do you balance your logical thinking with your intuitive feelings? Is one more predominant than the other? Why do you think this is so?

Does your intuition seem to have a spiritual source? Could you imagine that your intuition is Spirit guiding you to take one path when your left brain might be trying to get you to go down another? Is fear a factor in listening to your intuition? If so, do you know what you are afraid of?

The creative path is a journey into the unknown. When you start a beading project, do you always need to know what it is going to look like when it is finished before you even begin? If so, what do you think is preventing you from allowing yourself to play in the creative process and let go of your need to control every bead and every stitch? How is this tendency reflected externally in your life? How might you use your beading to explore new levels of trusting your intuition? Your Song needs the quality of intuition to be complete.

10. Happiness

Each of us decides what happiness means to us. Something does not "make" us happy; rather, happiness is a state of being inside of us that we can connect with whenever we choose. Part of Joseph Campbell's advice to "follow your bliss" means finding happiness and staying connected with it, no matter how hard external forces have tried to disconnect you from it.

The dictionary defines *bliss* as "serene happiness" and "spiritual joy." I would say it is a heightened feeling of joy and happiness combined together when we are singing our Song. Perhaps happiness can make a positive contribution to our health as well. When we are beading our bliss, we are not in a state of anger, stress, or feeling uptight—all conditions that contribute to various forms of ill health. I have had students who have turned to their beading to help them get through cancer treatments because beading allowed them to feel some measure of joy and happiness. Perhaps a new slogan for beaders could be, "Don't worry, bead happy!"

Song Bead 10.

Many people are happiest when they are engaged in a creative act, either as an active participant or as an observer. Sometimes I am as happy beading as when I am witnessing a beautiful sunset or a magical moonrise over water. The completion of a month-long beading project stirs up as much joy and happiness in me as the golden aspen trees shimmering on a fall day in the Colorado high country. In both instances my soul is affected by what I would term a spiritual release of energy that comes from feeling connected to my inner happiness, joy, and bliss.

How do you find happiness in your creative process? Does it come "automatically" when you sit down and start to work with all your colorful beads? Do you feel happy when you complete a project? Have you ever felt a shift inside of you while beading that produced a blissful state of being? Can you say that you "bead your bliss"? If not, can you sense what is blocking you?

If you are "beading your bliss," can you see how the happiness you feel while beading radiates out into the rest of your life? Is it noticeable to your friends and family? My hope is that the happiness you experience while singing your Song impacts your whole life, inner and outer, and that its effects will flow out from you, helping make our world a better place for all.

◎◎◎

Having examined the ten beads of our Song, it is now time to string them together and wear them with grace and humility. When you embody the tools of your creativity, they will serve you well on your journey through life, whatever your destination is.

My hope is that beading your bliss, singing your Song will open up the doors to the Creative Spirit and allow the river of infinite possibilities to begin flowing through you. You do not need to push it because it flows by itself! Grab your beads, get to work, and let the current carry you along on your life's journey. I will meet you in that field Rumi spoke of, out beyond all ideas of right-doing and wrong-doing. We will sit under the shade of an acacia tree with our beads to sing our Songs in unison and harmony. Will you join me there?

Before you begin Project 13, I want to offer an exercise in examining the qualities of your own unique Song. Identifying and connecting with the way you use these ten innate qualities can help you discover and express your own original Song.

E XERCISE

Discovering Your Song

You will need ten sheets of paper and a pencil or pen for this exercise.

1. At the top of each sheet, write the following qualities, one per sheet:
   - Passion
   - Persistence

- Commitment
- Freedom
- Wholeness
- Vision
- Integrity
- Authenticity
- Intuition
- Happiness

2. Taking each quality one at a time, make a list of all the ways you connect with that particular quality in your life at this time in your life.

3. You can use the Sacred Triangle and the positions of each of the Asker, the Witness, and the Experiencer to help you in this exercise. (Refer to chapter 3, p. 76) First ask the question, How is this quality reflected in my life? (the Asker). Then move into the position of witnessing how this quality is reflected in your life (the Witness). When you get the experience of how it is reflected in your life, write it down on the paper (the Experiencer).

4. When you have considered each of the ten qualities, ask yourself if there are any other qualities that assist you in singing your Song. Write them on another piece of paper and take some time to reflect on them, as well.

PROJECT 13
Song Beads

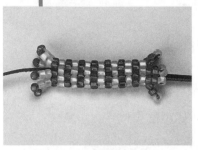

Song Bead, gourd stitch beaded tube bead, Wendy Ellsworth, 2009. (For a color photograph of this project, see color plate 8a.)

Beaded beads are a fun way to practice learning different beading techniques. Here is a fun beaded tube bead I designed using flat weave gourd stitch. The bead is first woven flat then "zipped" up, which brings it into a tubular shape. By changing the colors and sizes of the beads, you can make many variations of this Song Bead. Then you can string them all together to make a Song Bead Necklace.

MATERIALS

- Japanese seed beads, size 8, in two contrasting colors, 2 grams each color
- Silamide thread size A or Nymo size B, to match one bead color
- Sharps short beading needles, size 10
- Scissors
- Beading mat
- Ott light or desk lamp

PROJECT PREPARATION

- Pull off 10 feet of thread and prestretch it by pulling it out between your hands, working your way along its entire length.
- Add a needle to your thread, pulling it to the center of the thread. You will work with a double thread.
- Add a "stop" bead onto the thread, locating it approximately 14 inches from the ends of the threads. (The "stop" bead prevents the base row of beads from falling off the thread.)

- Pass back through the stop bead two more times, being careful not to bisect the threads in doing so because you will need to pull it off eventually.

Base Row (Rows 1 and 2)

(see figure 7.1)

- Pick up a total of fourteen beads, alternating color 1 and color 2. Pick up one bead of color 1, one bead of color 2, and repeat until you have all fourteen on the thread.
- Run your beads down to the stop bead. (Figure 7.1 also shows the first bead of row 3 (bead 15) on the needle ready to begin row 3.)

Row 3

(see figure 7.2)

- Working only in color 2, pick up a bead, skip a bead in the base row, and stitch into the next bead in the base row. Every bead you stitch into will be a color 1 bead. (Figure 7.2 shows the first bead of row 4 (bead 22) on the needle ready for the next stitch.)

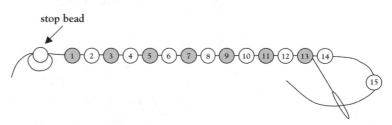

7.1. Tube bead, rows 1 and 2.

Row 4

(see figure 7.3)

- Working only in color 1, place a bead in between every bead of row 3.

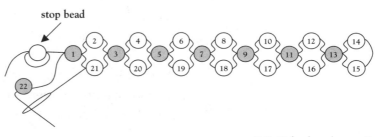

7.2. Tube bead, row 3.

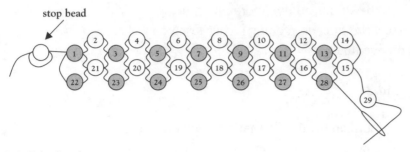

7.3. Tube bead, row 4.

Every bead you stitch into will be a color 2 bead. (Figure 7.3 shows the first bead of row 5 (bead 29) on the needle ready for the next stitch.)

Row 5

- Working only in color 2, place a bead in between every bead of row 4. Every bead you stitch into will be a color 1 bead.

Rows 6–14

- Repeat rows 4 and 5, alternating colors each row. Your final row will be in color 1. You will have a total of seven rows of color 1 and seven rows of color 2.

Zipping Up the Bead

- Bring the two edges of the beaded tube bead together lengthwise. You will notice that the color 2 beads from row 2 will fit right between the color 1 beads of row 14.
- Using your working thread, stitch or "zip" these two edges together, going from a color 1 bead to a color 2 bead, zig-zagging, until you reach the opposite edge.
- For extra strength, stitch back through these beads again in the opposite direction.
- Your working thread will now be coming out of a bead on the opposite end of your new beaded tube bead from the starting thread tails.
- Your beaded tube bead is now complete unless you want to add an additional embellishment to both ends of it. If so, skip "Ending the Thread" and go to "Fringe Embellishment."

Ending the Thread

- Make two slip knots around the thread that connects the bead your thread is coming out of and the next bead beside it at the end of your tube. Stitch into several additional beads and cut off the thread.
- Repeat this at the other end of the tube bead, adding a needle onto the thread tails in order to do this.

Fringe Embellishment

(see figure 7.4)

There are many types of possible fringe embellishment that you could use at the ends of your beaded tube bead. Here are directions for one that I like to use:

- Your working thread must be coming out of one of the beads at the end of the beaded tube. Pick up three beads in any color sequence and bring them down to the end of the thread. Pass back through the first two beads added and back into the same bead your thread is coming out of.
- Stitch into the next end bead and repeat the directions above.
- Continue to add a three-bead fringe embellishment at the end of each bead of the tube bead. You will have a total of seven of these embellishments.
- End your working thread.
- Add a needle onto the thread tails at the opposite end of the tube bead and repeat the same directions; then end your thread.

⊙⊙⊙

You have just made a "beaded" tube bead! You can string it onto a chain to wear around your neck, or you can bead a number of them and string them all up together for your Song Bead Necklace.

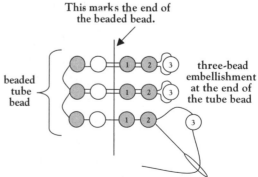

This marks the end of the beaded bead.

beaded tube bead

three-bead embellishment at the end of the tube bead

7.4. Three-bead fringe embellishment.

Before you begin Project 14, I recommend that you take a few moments to invite beauty into your work through this meditation.

Meditation
Beauty

The ability to experience beauty is one of the greatest gifts of being human. May you be the beauty you feel internally and may this beauty radiate out until it fills the Song of your life.

1. Find a place where you can sit undisturbed for awhile.
2. Sit with your spine straight and feet on the floor if you are in a chair.
3. Take three deep breaths, releasing any tension you are holding with each exhalation.
4. Be sure to relax your jaw, your shoulders, your brow, and your tongue.
5. Bring your attention to your breath, noticing the inhalation and the exhalation.
6. Let the chatter of your "monkey mind" fade away; keep focusing on your breath.
7. Visualize a scene in a natural setting where you are surrounded by beauty.
8. Enjoy the sense of peace and healing that is inherent in this natural scene.
9. Focus on the beauty you are experiencing and invite it to come into your Heart chakra. Fill your heart until it is overflowing with beauty's radiant energy.
10. Now bring the feeling of peace into your heart, filling it up with its calming energy and feeling protected and safe from any harm.

11. Breathe gently into the beauty and peace that are now inside your loving heart space. Let your heart expand as you hold the vision of beauty and peace there.

12. Breathe in beauty, breathe out beauty. Breathe in peace, breathe out peace.

13. Feel yourself expand into a state of grace as you breathe beauty and peace in and out.

14. Repeat this until you are ready to end your meditation.

15. End your meditation by thanking Mother Nature for the gifts of beauty and peace she has given you.

16. Open your eyes and know that the beauty and peace you have filled up your heart with will continue to illuminate and charge you with their positive, calming energies throughout the rest of your day.

PROJECT 14
Herringbone Stitch
Cuff with Freshwater Pearls

Here is a final project for you to make that is a reflection of my personal bead Song. In designing this cuff, I utilized all ten of the qualities described previously. If you choose to embellish it, the cuff will look as if it is a mini coral reef wrapped around your wrist, radiating beauty all on its own. It is made using the versatile herringbone stitch from the Ndebele people of South Africa.

Herringbone Stitch Cuff with Freshwater Pearls, herringbone stitch, unembellished, Wendy Ellsworth, 2008. (For a color photograph of this project, see color plate 8b.)

MATERIALS

- Matsuno seed beads, size 8, in your color choice, approximately 25 grams
- Matsuno seed beads, size 11, in same color choice, approximately forty beads
- Czech seed beads, size 11, for fringe embellishment, one hank (or multiple colors)
- Japanese seed beads, size 15, for tips of embellishment fringe, 5 grams
- Eight freshwater side-drilled potato pearls, size 4–4.5 millimeters
- Forty-eight freshwater side-drilled button pearls, size 1.5–2.00 millimeters
- Silamide thread size A, to match seed bead color
- Button with shank
- Scissors
- Beading mat
- Ott light or desk lamp

- *Note:* It is important to the design of this cuff that you use Japanese Matsuno seed beads. If necessary, look in the Resources section at the back of the book for bead purveyors who sell them.

PROJECT PREPARATION

- Pull off approximately 9 feet of thread and prestretch.
- Add your needle to the thread and bring it to the middle of your thread to work the thread doubled. Do not tie off the ends of the threads.

Base Row (Two-Bead Ladder Stitch)

- Using the size-8 Matsuno seed beads, make a two-bead ladder fifty-two units in length, leaving a 4-inch tail to be woven in later. (Refer to chapter 2, Project 4 for two-bead ladder stitch directions, figures 2.1 through 2.5.)
- Measure this length on your wrist to see if you need to either subtract beads or add more on to get the right length to fit you. You want the total length to just meet when you wrap it around your wrist. You need to keep the count to an even number of beads, however, so if you need to add or subtract from the fifty-two units, add or subtract in units of two.
- Make a second two-bead ladder the same length and put it aside for now.

Row 1 (Herringbone Stitch)

You will be working in herringbone stitch off of the two-bead ladder base. You will do this in two steps (see figure 7.5):

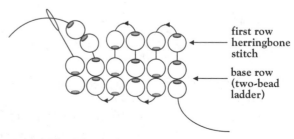

> Step 1: Pick up two beads and stitch down into the next two-bead unit in the ladder base row.

> Step 2: Stitch back up through the next two-bead unit in the ladder base row.

first row herringbone stitch

base row (two-bead ladder)

7.5. Starting herringbone stitch off two-bead ladder base.

Repeat these two steps along the length of your ladder base to the other end.

Making a Turn
(see figure 7.6)

- At the end of the row, make a turn so that your needle and thread are in position to begin row 2. To do this, stitch down into both beads of the ladder base in your final stitch of row 1; then bring your needle and thread up through the second two-bead ladder stitch (from the outer edge) from bottom to top and through the top outer edge bead in row 1

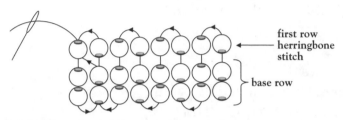

first row herringbone stitch

base row

7.6. Making a turn at the end of a row to be in position for next row.

from bottom to top. (In figure 7.6 the arrows at the bottom left side show you the thread path for this turn.)

- Your thread and needle are now in position to begin the next row of herringbone stitch. You always want to make a turn at the end of each row in this manner, though you will only go down to the base row this one time.
- On each subsequent row, stitch down only one bead to start the turn.

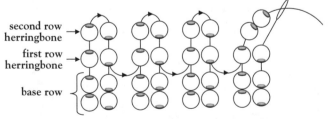

second row herringbone

first row herringbone

base row

7.7. Thread path of second row of herringbone stitch.

Rows 2 and 3
(see figure 7.7)

- Work in herringbone stitch. The rhythm for this stitch is: pick up two beads, stitch down one, up one. This is what forms the characteristic "herringbone" pattern, where you have two beads sitting on top of two beads at an angle.

- Make a turn at the end of each row to be in position to begin a subsequent row.

Row 4

Note: These directions are based on a base row count of fifty-two units in length, which equals twenty-six total stitches in herringbone across the row. I will refer to each two-bead herringbone stitch as an "HU" (herringbone unit).

- Work six HUs in herringbone stitch.
- Between the sixth and seventh HU, place a single 1.5-millimeter button freshwater pearl as an increase bead. To do this, pick up the two beads for the sixth HU and stitch down into the bead below. Pick up a single freshwater pearl and stitch up into the seventh HU. (See figure 7.8.)

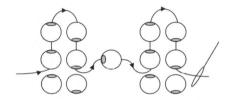

7.8. Single pearl increase.

- If you increased the initial base row count to fifty-six units, you would place the first pearl in between the seventh and eighth HU. That will give you seven herringbone stitches (HUs) at both ends. If you only increased the initial count to fifty-four units, you would still place the first pearl increase between the sixth and seventh HU. There will be six stitches at one end and seven at the opposite end.
- Repeat this increase in between every other HU for a total of eight pearls in this row.
- Work the final six HUs in herringbone stitch to finish the row and make your turn.

Row 5

- In this row, when you get to where you placed a single pearl in row 4, place a two-pearl increase in the gap between the HUs. Do not stitch into the single pearl increase of row 5; it just sits there all by itself. (See figure 7.9.)

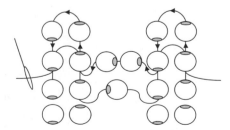

7.9. Two-pearl increase.

- Work the final six HUs in herringbone stitch to finish the row and make your turn.

Row 6

- Work 6 HUs in herringbone stitch.
- When you come to the two-pearl increases, place a 4.4-millimeter potato freshwater pearl in the gap over the top of the two-pearl increase. Do not stitch back into the two-pearl increases.
- Add the button with clasp in between the next to last and final HU. To do this, simply pass your needle and thread through the shank of the button in the gap between the last and final HU before stitching into the final HU.
- Complete your final HU and make your turn.

Row 7

- Work the first HU and pass your needle back through the button shank a second time before you stitch into the second HU.
- Work each HU in herringbone stitch *and* when you get to the large pearls from row 7, stitch back through them a second time. To do this, pick up two beads, stitch down one bead, pass back through the pearl, and stitch up one bead.
- Make your turn.

Row 8

- Repeat row 5, keeping a tight thread tension.

Row 9

- Repeat row 4, keeping a tight thread tension.

Row 10

- Work in herringbone stitch, keeping a tight thread tension to pull the cuff back into alignment. Make a turn so that the working thread is coming out of the top edge bead just as if you were starting another row of herringbone.

Joining Second Two-Bead Ladder Strip to Herringbone Cuff
(see figure 7.10)

- Join the second two-bead ladder strip to the rest of the cuff by stitching into it bead by bead. To do this, stitch up into the two beads on one of the outer edges of the ladder strip; then stitch back down through the next two beads of the ladder strip and the next bead in the herringbone cuff.
- Bring your needle over to the next "up" stitch in the herringbone cuff and repeat. (The arrows in figure 7.10 show you the thread path.)

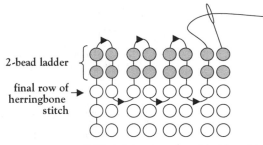

7.10. Joining two-bead ladder strip to herringbone cuff.

Adding Loop for Button Clasp
(see figure 7.11)

- Add on a new double thread so that it exits from bead 7 in figure 7.11.
- Pick up two size-8 Matsuno seed beads (A and B in figure 7.11) and enough size-11 Matsuno seed beads to fit around the button.
- Stitch back through B, pick up one more size-8 Matsuno seed bead (C in figure 7.11).
- Stitch into the next bead in sequence in the cuff (bead 8 in figure 7.11).
- Weave the thread around so that you can make a second pass through the entire loop.

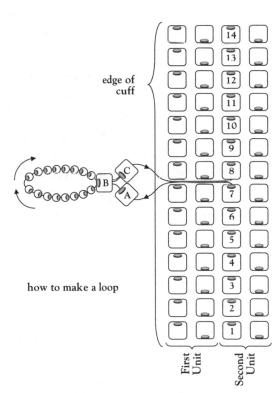

7.11. Adding loop for button clasp.

- Tie a knot to secure the thread before cutting it off.
- Weave in the tail of the starting thread.

FINISHING
(2 options)

Option 1: Picot edge embellishment
(refer to chapter 4, figure 4.7)

- If you want a simple three-bead picot as an edging embellishment, add on a new thread so that it comes out of the first bead at one end of an edge.
- Pick up three size-11 beads in a contrasting or complimentary color and pass your needle down through the next two-bead column and up through the subsequent two-bead column to get back to the top of the edge.
- Repeat, adding three beads for a picot edging all along both edges of the cuff.

Option 2: Coral reef fringe embellishment
If you want to add fringe to the entire cuff, it will turn it into a dazzling mini coral reef form to wear on your wrist. A word of caution: it takes a very long time to do this! This amount of embellishment fringe more than doubles the time it takes to make the cuff itself. Remember, each bead you pick up and each stitch you take is simply where you are at this moment in time. Have fun and "Bead happy"! If you choose to continue:

- Put a three- or four-bead fringe of size-11 Czech seed beads, capped with a size-15 seed bead, between every size-8 bead of the cuff, including along the edges. (See color plate 8b.)
- To do this, add on a new thread so that it comes out of an end bead of the two-bead ladder on one side of the cuff.
- Pick up three or four size-11 Czech seed beads plus one size-15 seed bead and pass them back through the Czech beads and the size-8 end bead. Your needle should now be coming out of the center of the first two-bead ladder stitch.

- Pick up the next fringe beads, pass back through the Czech seed beads, and stitch into next size-8 bead in your vertical column.
- Keep adding individual fringe beads in and out of every bead in the vertical column; then start down the next column. (I leave empty spaces where the loop needs to lay flat as well as underneath the button clasp.)
- When you have added a fringe embellishment between every size-8 bead in your cuff, you are finished!

◎◎◎

Wear your Herringbone Stitch Cuff and enjoy the beauty that is wrapped around your wrist! Let the beauty that is reflected in this piece of bead art be a reminder of the beauty that surrounds you in the natural world. Let it also be a reflection of your sacred center, the beautiful core of who you are intrinsically.

INSPIRATION FOR THE FUTURE: CREATING A BEAD CHALLENGE

I want to leave you with a final inspiration to use as you move forward with your beading. I invite you to create mini "bead challenges" for yourself. The following are suggestions that you can use anytime you feel the need to break out of a rut you find yourself in and cannot seem to get out of. Sometimes you may need to push yourself in order to break out of an old mold that once served you well but has become restrictive to new growth and change. This holds true in all areas of your life and especially in your creative life.

You may want to keep a journal for your thoughts, emotions, and feelings as you process through a challenge you have set up. Be especially aware of any shift in consciousness that may occur as you participate in your bead challenge. Notice how it affects you in other parts of your life. Set the intention to stretch yourself in ways you have not done before, and watch what happens as a result.

Here are some ideas for ways you can create your bead challenge:

- Decide to learn a new stitch you have not tried before and design something to make using the stitch.
- Try combining several stitches into one project and see how that affects the design of what you make.
- Decide to "shake up" your color palette by deliberately using a color palette that is very different from your usual color comfort zone.
- If you have never worked three-dimensionally, try making a sculptural form that is 3-D.
- Try combining different sizes of beads in one piece.
- If you have never done a particular stitch free-form, try it and see what happens. See where it leads you and what you learn from it.
- Sign up for a class with a teacher you have always wanted to study with but have not because you did not think you had the time or the money or the expertise or whatever other excuse you have used.
- Set up a bead retreat with some of your "beady" friends and do one of these ideas together as a group exercise.
- Decide to make a piece for one of the bead challenges that might be offered through a bead society or *Bead & Button* magazine.
- Create a Bead Song Necklace by making a beaded bead for each of the ten beads of our Song.
- Use your creative imagination to come up with a bead challenge that will stretch your beading skills.

Each day is a new opportunity to find your sacred center through the art of beadwork. It is my hope that these challenges will help you grow and change whenever you feel the need. Beading can be the key that opens the door to being able to fully sing your Song. May it be so.

RESOURCES

Bead Purveyors

Bead Cats: www.beadcats.com (Virginia Blakelock, Carol Perrenoud)

    Czech glass seed beads

    Czech molded beads

    Beading needles: Sharps short beading size 12 and 10

    Silamide thread

Bead Room: www.beadroom.com (Laura Chatain)

    Japanese Matsuno seed beads

    Czech seed beads

    Czech pressed-glass leaves and flowers

Beads by Blanche: www.beadsbyblanche.com

    Japanese and Czech seed beads

    Pearls

    Vintage beads

Beyond Beadery: www.beyondbeadery.com (Betcey Ventrella)

    Japanese Matsuno, Miyuki, and Toho seed beads

    Czech seed beads

    Silamide thread

    Beading needles: Sharps short beading size 12 and 10

Creative Castle: www.creativecastle.com

    Japanese seed beads

    Vintage glass

    Swarovski crystals

Crystal Creations: www.BeadsGoneWild.com

    Full bead store

Fire Mountain Gems: www.firemountaingems.com
> Large vendor of beads and jewelry supplies.

General Bead: www.genbead.com
> Czech seed beads

> Japanese Matsuno seed beads

My Father's Beads: www.myfathersbeads.com (Jeri Bellini Smith)
> Japanese seed beads

> Findings

> Tools

Shipwreck Beads: www.shipwreck-beads.com
> Czech True Cut faceted seed beads, size 10

Stormcloud Trading Co: www.beadstorm.com
> Japanese beads

> Czech beads

> Swarovski crystals

Webs America's Bead Store: www.websbeads.com (Barbara Weiss)
> Vendor of beads and jewelry supplies.

Bead Magazines

Bead & Button: www.beadandbutton.com

Beadwork: www.beadworkmagazine.com

Sources for Beading Substrate

Fields Fabrics: http://fieldsfabrics.com
> Ultrasuede

Robin Atkins: www.robinatkins.com
> Acid-free interleaving paper

Sova Enterprises: www.sova-enterprises.com/catalog
> Bead backing

Recommended Books for Off-Loom Bead Weaving Basics

Cypher, Carol Huber. *Mastering Beadwork: A Comprehensive Guide to Off-Loom Techniques.* Loveland, CO: Interweave Press, 2007.

Wedekind, Dustin. *Getting Started with Seed Beads.* Loveland, CO: Interweave Press, 2007.

Wells, Carol Wilcox. *Creative Bead Weaving: A Contemporary Guide to Classic Off-Loom Stitches.* Asheville, NC: Lark Books, 1996.

BIBLIOGRAPHY

Allen, Pat B. *Art Is a Way of Knowing: A Guide to Self-Knowledge and Spiritual Fulfillment through Creativity*. Boston: Shambhala, 1995.

Andrews, Ted. *How to Heal with Color*. Woodbury, MN: Llewellyn, 2001.

Apostolos-Cappadona, Diane, ed. *Art, Creativity, and the Sacred: An Anthology in Religion and Art*. New York: Crossroad, 1984.

Arewa, Caroline Shola. *Opening to Spirit: Contacting the Healing Power of the Chakras and Honoring African Spirituality*. London: HarperCollins, 1998.

Arguelles, Jose. *The Mayan Factor: Path Beyond Technology*. Santa Fe: Bear, 1987.

Arguelles, Jose, and Miriam. *Mandala*. Berkeley, CA: Shambala, 1972.

Arrien, Angeles. *Signs of Life: The Five Universal Shapes and How to Use Them*. Sonoma, CA: Arcus, 1992.

Azara, Nancy. *Spirit Taking Form: Making a Spiritual Practice of Making Art*. York Beach, ME: Red Wheel/Weiser, 2002.

Beam, Mary Todd. *Celebrate Your Creative Self: More Than 25 Exercises to Unleash the Artist Within*. Cincinnati: North Light Books, 2001.

Benesh, Carolyn L. E. "Fashion in Colors: 300 Years of Historic and Contemporary Costume." *Ornament* 2 (2005):51–55.

Bolen, Jean Shinoda. *Goddesses in Older Women: Archetypes in Women Over Fifty*. New York: HarperCollins, 2001.

Braden, Gregg. *Secrets of the Lost Mode of Prayer: The Hidden Power of Beauty, Blessings, Wisdom, and Heart*. Carlsbad, CA: Hay House, 2006.

———. *Walking between the Worlds: The Science of Compassion*. Bellevue, WA: Radio Bookstore Press, 1997.

Brennan, Barbara Ann. *Hands of Light: A Guide to Healing through the Human Energy Field*. New York: Bantam Books, 1988.

———. *Light Emerging: The Journey of Personal Healing*. New York: Bantam Books, 1993.

Campbell, Don G. *The Roar of Silence: Healing Powers of Breath, Tone, and Music.* Wheaton, IL: The Theosophical Publishing House, 1989.

Campbell, Joseph. *The Power of Myth.* With Bill Moyers. New York: Doubleday, 1988.

Clark, Linda. *The Ancient Art of Color Therapy.* New York: Simon & Schuster, 1975.

Cook, Jeannette. *Beady Eyed Women's Guide to Exquisite Beading: A Peyote Projects Primer.* Lemon Grove, CA: Beady Eyed Women's Guides, 1996.

Cooper, J. C. *An Illustrated Encyclopedia of Traditional Symbols.* London: Thames and Hudson, 1978.

Cornell, Judith. *Mandala: Luminous Symbols for Healing.* Wheaton, IL: Quest Books, 1994.

Dass, Ram. *Be Here Now.* New York: Brown Books, 1971.

Deeb, Margie. *The Beader's Color Palette.* New York: Watson-Guptill, 2008.

———. *The Beader's Guide to Color.* New York: Watson-Guptill, 2004.

Dubin, Lois Sherr. *The History of Beads: From 30,000 B.C. to the Present.* New York: Abrams, 1987.

Dyer, Wayne. *Your Erroneous Zones.* New York: Avon Books, 1976.

Eha, Nancy. *Off the Beadin' Path: Discovering Your Own Creative Trail of Bead Embellishment.* St. Paul: Creative Visions Press, 1997.

Estés, Clarissa Pinkola. *Women Who Run with the Wolves: Myths and Stories of the Wild Woman Archetype.* New York: Ballantine Books, 1992.

Fincher, Susanne F. *Creating Mandalas: For Insight, Healing, and Self-Expression.* Boston: Shambhala, 1991.

Fox, Matthew. *Creativity: Where the Divine and the Human Meet.* New York: Tarcher/Penguin, 2002.

Ganim, Barbara. *Art and Healing: Using Expressive Art to Heal Your Body, Mind, and Spirit.* New York: Three Rivers Press, 1999.

Gendlin, Eugene T. *Focusing.* New York: Bantam Books, 1981.

Gimbutas, Marija. *The Goddesses and Gods of Old Europe: Myths and Cult Images.* Berkeley, CA: University of California Press, 1992.

Judith, Anodea. *Wheels of Life: A User's Guide to the Chakra System.* Woodbury, MN: Llewellyn, 2008.

Kahn, Barry, ed. *Myths and Folk Tales: Selections from the Second International Miyuki Delica Challenge.* Portland, ME: Caravan Beads, 2000.

Kaplan-Williams, Strephon. *Transforming Childhood: A Handbook for Personal Growth.* Berkeley, CA: Journey Press, 1988.

Koren, Leonard. *Wabi Sabi: For Artists, Designers, Poets and Philosophers.* Berkeley, CA: Stone Bridge Press, 1994.

Leadbeater, C. W. *The Chakras*. Wheaton, IL: The Theosophical Publishing House, 1927.

Liberman, Jacob. *Light: Medicine of the Future*. Rochester, VT: Bear, 1991.

Mander, Jerry. *In the Absence of the Sacred: The Failure of Technology and the Survival of the Indian Nations*. San Francisco: Sierra Club Books, 1991.

Mann, Rhodia. *Talk to the Stars: The Samburu of Northern Kenya*. Nairibi, Kenya: Desert Sands, 2005.

Marciniak, Barbara. *Bringers of the Dawn*. Santa Fe: Bear, 1992.

McLean, Adam. *The Alchemical Mandala: A Survey of the Mandala in the Western Esoteric Traditions*. Grand Rapids, MI: Phanes Press, 1989.

Menz, Deb. *ColorWorks: The Crafter's Guide to Color*. Loveland, CO: Interweave Press, 2004.

Myss, Caroline. *Anatomy of the Spirit: The Seven Stages of Power and Healing*. New York: Harmony Books, 1996.

———. *Sacred Contracts: Awakening Your Divine Potential*. New York: Harmony Books, 2001.

Nachmanovitch, Stephen. *Free Play: Improvisation in Life and Art*. New York: Tarcher/Putnam, 1990.

Piepenburg, Robert. *Treasures of the Creative Spirit: An Artist's Understanding of Human Creativity*. Farmington Hills, MI: Pebble Press, 1998.

Purce, Jill. *The Mystic Spiral: Journey of the Soul*. London: Thames & Hudson, 1974.

Richards, M. C. *Centering: In Pottery, Poetry, and the Person*. Middletown, CT: Wesleyan University Press, 1962.

Scott, Joyce J. *Fearless Beadwork: Handwriting and Drawings from Hell*. Rochester, NY: Visual Studies Workshop & Mid-Atlantic Arts Foundation, 1994.

Smith, Huston. *The Illustrated World's Religions: A Guide to Our Wisdom Paths*. San Francisco: HarperCollins, 1995.

Taylor, Jill. *My Stroke of Insight: A Brain Scientist's Personal Journey*. New York: Viking, 2008.

Tolle, Eckart. *A New Earth: Awakening to Your Life's Purpose*. New York: Penguin Group, 2005.

———. *The Power of Now: A Guide to Spiritual Enlightenment*. Novato, CA: New World Library, 1999.

Wallace, Sandra. *The Beader's Color Mixing Directory*. Iola, WI: Krause, 2007.

Ward, Geoff. *Spirals: The Pattern of Existence*. Somerset, UK: Green Magic, 2006.

Wauters, Ambika. *The Book of Chakras*. London: Quarto, 2002.

Wells, Carol Wilcox, ed. *Masters: Beadweaving*. New York: Lark Books, 2008.

Whitaker, Kay Cordell. *The Reluctant Shaman*. New York: HarperCollins, 1991.

———. *Sacred Link*. Santa Fe: The Writer's Collective, 2005.

Wiley, Eleanor, and Maggie Oman Shannon. *A String and a Prayer: How to Make and Use Prayer Beads*. York Beach, ME: Red Wheel/Weiser, 2002.

Wilshire, Donna. *Virgin Mother Crone: Myths and Mysteries of the Triple Goddess*. Rochester, VT: Inner Traditions, 1994.

Winston, Kimberly. *Bead One, Pray Too: A Guide to Making and Using Prayer Beads*. New York: Moorehouse, 2008.

Wuthnow, Robert. *Creative Spirituality: The Way of the Artist*. Berkeley, CA: University of California Press, 2001.

Zajonc, Arthur. *Catching the Light: The Entwined History of Light and Mind*. New York: Bantam Books, 1993.

Project Index

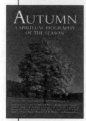

Spirituality of the Seasons

Autumn: A Spiritual Biography of the Season
Edited by Gary Schmidt and Susan M. Felch; Illustrations by Mary Azarian
Rejoice in autumn as a time of preparation and reflection. Includes Wendell Berry, David James Duncan, Robert Frost, A. Bartlett Giamatti, E. B. White, P. D. James, Julian of Norwich, Garret Keizer, Tracy Kidder, Anne Lamott, May Sarton.
6 x 9, 320 pp, 5 b/w illus., Quality PB, 978-1-59473-118-1 **$18.99**

Spring: A Spiritual Biography of the Season
Edited by Gary Schmidt and Susan M. Felch; Illustrations by Mary Azarian
Explore the gentle unfurling of spring and reflect on how nature celebrates rebirth and renewal. Includes Jane Kenyon, Lucy Larcom, Harry Thurston, Nathaniel Hawthorne, Noel Perrin, Annie Dillard, Martha Ballard, Barbara Kingsolver, Dorothy Wordsworth, Donald Hall, David Brill, Lionel Basney, Isak Dinesen, Paul Laurence Dunbar.
6 x 9, 352 pp, 6 b/w illus., Quality PB, 978-1-59473-246-1 **$18.99**

Summer: A Spiritual Biography of the Season
Edited by Gary Schmidt and Susan M. Felch; Illustrations by Barry Moser
"A sumptuous banquet.... These selections lift up an exquisite wholeness found within an everyday sophistication."— ★ *Publishers Weekly* starred review
Includes Anne Lamott, Luci Shaw, Ray Bradbury, Richard Selzer, Thomas Lynch, Walt Whitman, Carl Sandburg, Sherman Alexie, Madeleine L'Engle, Jamaica Kincaid.
6 x 9, 304 pp, 5 b/w illus., Quality PB, 978-1-59473-183-9 **$18.99**
HC, 978-1-59473-083-2 **$21.99**

Winter: A Spiritual Biography of the Season
Edited by Gary Schmidt and Susan M. Felch; Illustrations by Barry Moser
"This outstanding anthology features top-flight nature and spirituality writers on the fierce, inexorable season of winter.... Remarkably lively and warm, despite the icy subject." — ★ *Publishers Weekly* starred review
Includes Will Campbell, Rachel Carson, Annie Dillard, Donald Hall, Ron Hansen, Jane Kenyon, Jamaica Kincaid, Barry Lopez, Kathleen Norris, John Updike, E. B. White.
6 x 9, 288 pp, 6 b/w illus., Deluxe PB w/flaps, 978-1-893361-92-8 **$18.95**

Spirituality / Animal Companions

Blessing the Animals
Prayers and Ceremonies to Celebrate God's Creatures, Wild and Tame
Edited by Lynn L. Caruso
5¼ x 7¼, 256 pp, Quality PB, 978-1-59473-253-9 **$15.99**; HC, 978-1-59473-145-7 **$19.99**

Remembering My Pet
A Kid's Own Spiritual Workbook for When a Pet Dies
by Nechama Liss-Levinson, PhD, and Rev. Molly Phinney Baskette, MDiv; Foreword by Lynn L. Caruso
8 x 10, 48 pp, 2-color text, HC, 978-1-59473-221-3 **$16.99**

What Animals Can Teach Us about Spirituality
Inspiring Lessons from Wild and Tame Creatures
by Diana L. Guerrero
6 x 9, 176 pp, Quality PB, 978-1-893361-84-3 **$16.95**

Or phone, fax, mail or e-mail to: SKYLIGHT PATHS Publishing
Sunset Farm Offices, Route 4 • P.O. Box 237 • Woodstock, Vermont 05091
Tel: (802) 457-4000 • Fax: (802) 457-4004 • www.skylightpaths.com
Credit card orders: (800) 962-4544 (8:30AM–5:30PM ET Monday–Friday)
Generous discounts on quantity orders. SATISFACTION GUARANTEED. Prices subject to change.

Spirituality

Claiming Earth as Common Ground: The Ecological Crisis through the Lens of Faith *by Andrea Cohen-Kiener; Foreword by Rev. Sally Bingham*
Inspires us to work across denominational lines in order to fulfill our sacred imperative to care for God's creation. 6 x 9, 192 pp, Quality PB, 978-1-59473-261-4 **$16.99**

The Losses of Our Lives: The Sacred Gifts of Renewal in Everyday Loss
by Dr. Nancy Copeland-Payton
Reframes loss from the perspective that our everyday losses help us learn what we need to handle the major losses. 6 x 9, 176 pp (est), HC, 978-1-59473-271-3 **$19.99**

The Workplace and Spirituality: New Perspectives on Research and Practice *Edited by Dr. Joan Marques, Dr. Satinder Dhiman and Dr. Richard King*
Explores the benefits of workplace spirituality in making work more meaningful and rewarding. 6 x 9, 256 pp, HC, 978-1-59473-260-7 **$29.99**

A Spirituality for Brokenness: Discovering Your Deepest Self in Difficult Times *by Terry Taylor*
Guides you through a compassionate yet highly practical process of facing, accepting, and finally integrating your brokenness into your life—a process that can ultimately bring mending. 6 x 9, 176 pp, Quality PB, 978-1-59473-229-4 **$16.99**

Next to Godliness: Finding the Sacred in Housekeeping
Edited and with Introductions by Alice Peck
Offers new perspectives on how we can reach out for the Divine.
6 x 9, 224 pp, Quality PB, 978-1-59473-214-0 **$19.99**

Bread, Body, Spirit: Finding the Sacred in Food
Edited and with Introductions by Alice Peck
Explores how food feeds our faith. 6 x 9, 224 pp, Quality PB, 978-1-59473-242-3 **$19.99**

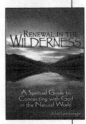

Renewal in the Wilderness: A Spiritual Guide to Connecting with God in the Natural World *by John Lionberger*
Reveals the power of experiencing God's presence in many variations of the natural world. 6 x 9, 176 pp, b/w photos, Quality PB, 978-1-59473-219-5 **$16.99**

Honoring Motherhood: Prayers, Ceremonies and Blessings
Edited and with Introductions by Lynn L. Caruso
Journey through the seasons of motherhood. 5 x 7¼, 272 pp, HC, 978-1-59473-239-3 **$19.99**

Soul Fire: Accessing Your Creativity *by Rev. Thomas Ryan, CSP*
Learn to cultivate your creative spirit. 6 x 9, 160 pp, Quality PB, 978-1-59473-243-0 **$16.99**

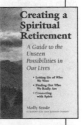

Money and the Way of Wisdom: Insights from the Book of Proverbs
by Timothy J. Sandoval, PhD 6 x 9, 192 pp, Quality PB, 978-1-59473-245-4 **$16.99**

Creating a Spiritual Retirement: A Guide to the Unseen Possibilities in Our Lives
by Molly Srode 6 x 9, 208 pp, b/w photos, Quality PB, 978-1-59473-050-4 **$14.99**
HC, 978-1-893361-75-1 **$19.95**

Finding Hope: Cultivating God's Gift of a Hopeful Spirit
by Marcia Ford 8 x 8, 200 pp, Quality PB, 978-1-59473-211-9 **$16.99**

Jewish Spirituality: A Brief Introduction for Christians *by Lawrence Kushner*
5½ x 8½, 112 pp, Quality PB, 978-1-58023-150-3 **$12.95** (A book from Jewish Lights, SkyLight Paths' sister imprint)

Journeys of Simplicity: Traveling Light with Thomas Merton, Bashō, Edward Abbey, Annie Dillard & Others *by Philip Harnden*
5 x 7¼, 144 pp, Quality PB, 978-1-59473-181-5 **$12.99** 128 pp, HC, 978-1-893361-76-8 **$16.95**

Keeping Spiritual Balance As We Grow Older: More than 65 Creative Ways to Use Purpose, Prayer, and the Power of Spirit to Build a Meaningful Retirement
by Molly and Bernie Srode 8 x 8, 224 pp, Quality PB, 978-1-59473-042-9 **$16.99**

Spiritually Incorrect: Finding God in All the *Wrong* Places *by Dan Wakefield; Illus. by Marian DelVecchio* 5½ x 8½, 192 pp, b/w illus., Quality PB, 978-1-59473-137-2 **$15.99**

A Walk with Four Spiritual Guides: Krishna, Buddha, Jesus, and Ramakrishna
by Andrew Harvey 5½ x 8½, 192 pp, 10 b/w photos & illus., Quality PB, 978-1-59473-138-9 **$15.99**

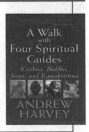

Spiritual Practice

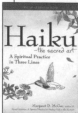

Haiku—The Sacred Art: A Spiritual Practice in Three Lines
by Margaret D. McGee Introduces haiku as a simple and effective way of tapping into the sacred moments that permeate everyday living.
5½ x 8½, 160 pp (est), Quality PB, 978-1-59473-269-0 **$16.99**

Dance—The Sacred Art: The Joy of Movement as a Spiritual Practice
by Cynthia Winton-Henry Invites all of us, regardless of experience, into the possibility of dance/movement as a spiritual practice.
5½ x 8½, 160 pp (est), Quality PB, 978-1-59473-268-3 **$16.99**

Spiritual Adventures in the Snow: Skiing & Snowboarding as Renewal for Your Soul *by Dr. Marcia McFee and Rev. Karen Foster; Foreword by Paul Arthur*
Explores snow sports as tangible experiences of the spiritual essence of our bodies and the earth. 5½ x 8½, 160 pp (est), Quality PB, 978-1-59473-270-6 **$16.99**

Recovery—The Sacred Art: The Twelve Steps as Spiritual Practice
by Rami Shapiro; Foreword by Joan Borysenko, PhD Uniquely interprets the Twelve Steps of Alcoholics Anonymous to speak to everyone seeking a freer and more God-centered life. 5½ x 8½, 240 pp, Quality PB, 978-1-59473-259-1 **$16.99**

Soul Fire: Accessing Your Creativity *by Rev. Thomas Ryan, CSP*
Shows you how to cultivate your creative spirit as a way to encourage personal growth.
6 x 9, 160 pp, Quality PB, 978-1-59473-243-0 **$16.99**

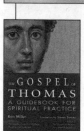

Running—The Sacred Art: Preparing to Practice
by Dr. Warren A. Kay; Foreword by Kristin Armstrong Examines how your daily run can enrich your spiritual life. 5½ x 8½, 160 pp, Quality PB, 978-1-59473-227-0 **$16.99**

Hospitality—The Sacred Art: Discovering the Hidden Spiritual Power of Invitation and Welcome *by Rev. Nanette Sawyer; Foreword by Rev. Dirk Ficca*
5½ x 8½, 192 pp, Quality PB, 978-1-59473-228-7 **$16.99**

Thanking & Blessing—The Sacred Art: Spiritual Vitality through Gratefulness
by Jay Marshall, PhD; Foreword by Philip Gulley 5½ x 8½, 176 pp, Quality PB, 978-1-59473-231-7 **$16.99**

Everyday Herbs in Spiritual Life: A Guide to Many Practices
by Michael J. Caduto; Foreword by Rosemary Gladstar
7 x 9, 208 pp, 21 b/w illustrations, Quality PB, 978-1-59473-174-7 **$16.99**

Divining the Body: Reclaim the Holiness of Your Physical Self *by Jan Phillips*
8 x 8, 256 pp, Quality PB, 978-1-59473-080-1 **$16.99**

The Gospel of Thomas: A Guidebook for Spiritual Practice
by Ron Miller; Translations by Stevan Davies 6 x 9, 160 pp, Quality PB, 978-1-59473-047-4 **$14.99**

Labyrinths from the Outside In: Walking to Spiritual Insight—A Beginner's Guide
by Donna Schaper and Carole Ann Camp
6 x 9, 208 pp, b/w illus. and photos, Quality PB, 978-1-893361-18-8 **$16.95**

Practicing the Sacred Art of Listening: A Guide to Enrich Your Relationships and Kindle Your Spiritual Life *by Kay Lindahl* 8 x 8, 176 pp, Quality PB, 978-1-893361-85-0 **$16.95**

The Sacred Art of Bowing: Preparing to Practice
by Andi Young 5½ x 8½, 128 pp, b/w illus., Quality PB, 978-1-893361-82-9 **$14.95**

The Sacred Art of Chant: Preparing to Practice
by Ana Hernández 5½ x 8½, 192 pp, Quality PB, 978-1-59473-036-8 **$15.99**

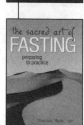

The Sacred Art of Fasting: Preparing to Practice
by Thomas Ryan, CSP 5½ x 8½, 192 pp, Quality PB, 978-1-59473-078-8 **$15.99**

The Sacred Art of Forgiveness: Forgiving Ourselves and Others through God's Grace
by Marcia Ford 8 x 8, 176 pp, Quality PB, 978-1-59473-175-4 **$16.99**

The Sacred Art of Listening: Forty Reflections for Cultivating a Spiritual Practice
by Kay Lindahl; Illustrations by Amy Schnapper
8 x 8, 160 pp, b/w illus., Quality PB, 978-1-893361-44-7 **$16.99**

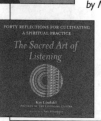

The Sacred Art of Lovingkindness: Preparing to Practice
by Rabbi Rami Shapiro; Foreword by Marcia Ford 5½ x 8½, 176 pp, Quality PB, 978-1-59473-151-8 **$16.99**

Sacred Speech: A Practical Guide for Keeping Spirit in Your Speech
by Rev. Donna Schaper 6 x 9, 176 pp, Quality PB, 978-1-59473-068-9 **$15.99**
HC, 978-1-893361-74-4 **$21.95**

Spirituality & Crafts

Contemplative Crochet
A Hands-On Guide for Interlocking Faith and Craft
by Cindy Crandall-Frazier; Foreword by Linda Skolnik

Illuminates the spiritual lessons you can learn through crocheting. Includes 10 original projects for beginners or experienced crocheters.

7 x 9, 208 pp, b/w photographs, Quality PB, 978-1-59473-238-6 **$16.99**

The Knitting Way
A Guide to Spiritual Self-Discovery
by Linda Skolnik and Janice MacDaniels

Examines how you can explore and strengthen your spiritual life through knitting. Includes 19 original knitting projects.

7 x 9, 240 pp, b/w photographs, Quality PB, 978-1-59473-079-5 **$16.99**

The Painting Path
Embodying Spiritual Discovery through Yoga, Brush and Color
by Linda Novick; Foreword by Richard Segalman

Explores the divine connection you can experience through creativity. Includes 11 step-by-step art projects accompanied by yoga-inspired exercises.

7 x 9, 208 pp, 8-page full-color insert, plus b/w photographs
Quality PB, 978-1-59473-226-3 **$18.99**

The Quilting Path
A Guide to Spiritual Discovery through Fabric, Thread and Kabbalah
by Louise Silk

Explores how to cultivate personal growth through quilt making. Includes 10 original quilting projects with dozens of variations.

7 x 9, 192 pp, b/w photographs and illustrations
Quality PB, 978-1-59473-206-5 **$16.99**

The Scrapbooking Journey
A Hands-On Guide to Spiritual Discovery
by Cory Richardson-Lauve; Foreword by Stacy Julian

Reveals how this craft can become a practice used to deepen and shape your life. Includes 8 original projects with dozens of variations.

7 x 9, 176 pp, 8-page full-color insert, plus b/w photographs
Quality PB, 978-1-59473-216-4 **$18.99**

The Soulwork of Clay
A Hands-On Approach to Spirituality
by Marjory Zoet Bankson; Photographs by Peter Bankson

Takes you through the seven-step process of making clay into a pot, drawing parallels at each stage to the process of spiritual growth. Includes a wealth of unique clay projects that even beginners can do.

7 x 9, 192 pp, b/w photographs, Quality PB, 978-1-59473-249-2 **$16.99**

About SKYLIGHT PATHS Publishing

SkyLight Paths Publishing is creating a place where people of different spiritual traditions come together for challenge and inspiration, a place where we can help each other understand the mystery that lies at the heart of our existence.

Through spirituality, our religious beliefs are increasingly becoming a part of our lives—rather than *apart* from our lives. While many of us may be more interested than ever in spiritual growth, we may be less firmly planted in traditional religion. Yet, we do want to deepen our relationship to the sacred, to learn from our own as well as from other faith traditions, and to practice in new ways.

SkyLight Paths sees both believers and seekers as a community that increasingly transcends traditional boundaries of religion and denomination—people wanting to learn from each other, *walking together, finding the way.*

For your information and convenience, at the back of this book we have provided a list of other SkyLight Paths books you might find interesting and useful. They cover the following subjects:

Buddhism / Zen	Global Spiritual	Monasticism
Catholicism	Perspectives	Mysticism
Children's Books	Gnosticism	Poetry
Christianity	Hinduism /	Prayer
Comparative	Vedanta	Religious Etiquette
Religion	Inspiration	Retirement
Current Events	Islam / Sufism	Spiritual Biography
Earth-Based	Judaism	Spiritual Direction
Spirituality	Kabbalah	Spirituality
Enneagram	Meditation	Women's Interest
	Midrash Fiction	Worship

Or phone, fax, mail or e-mail to: SKYLIGHT PATHS Publishing
Sunset Farm Offices, Route 4 • P.O. Box 237 • Woodstock, Vermont 05091
Tel: (802) 457-4000 • Fax: (802) 457-4004 • www.skylightpaths.com
Credit card orders: (800) 962-4544 (8:30AM–5:30PM ET Monday–Friday)
Generous discounts on quantity orders. SATISFACTION GUARANTEED. Prices subject to change.

For more information about each book,
visit our website at www.skylightpaths.com